THE Urban Cyclist's
SURVIVAL GUIDE

THE
Urban Cyclist's
SURVIVAL GUIDE

James Rubin & Scott Rowan

TRIUMPH
BOOKS

No part of this publication may be reproduced, stored in a retrieval system, or transmitted in any form by any means, electronic, mechanical, photocopying, or otherwise, without the prior written permission of the publisher, Triumph Books, 542 South Dearborn Street, Suite 750, Chicago, Illinois 60605.

Triumph Books and colophon are registered trademarks of Random House, Inc.

Library of Congress Cataloging-in-Publication Data
Rubin, James, 1960–
    Urban cyclist's survival guide / James Rubin and Scott Rowan.
        p. cm.
    ISBN 978-1-60078-566-5
1. Cycling—Handbooks, manuals, etc. 2. Bicycle commuting—
Handbooks, manuals, etc. 3. City traffic—Handbooks, manuals, etc.
I. Rowan, Scott, 1969– II. Title.
    GV1043.7.R83 2011
    796.6—dc22

                                                              2011014966

This book is available in quantity at special discounts for your group or organization. For further information, contact:

Triumph Books
542 South Dearborn Street
Suite 750
Chicago, Illinois 60605
(312) 939-3330
Fax (312) 663-3557
www.triumphbooks.com

Printed in U.S.A.

ISBN: 978-1-60078-566-5

Design by Sue Knopf

Unless otherwise noted, all photographs by Michal Czerwonka.

Contents

Preface

There is something brewing with bicycles and cities.

It's still small, but the signs of a movement are there. We see and hear anecdotally of more cyclists on roads in New York, Chicago, Los Angeles, and other cities. By cyclists, we don't mean the fancy, clip shoes set, out on 50-mile weekend jaunts. We mean people like us, wearing regular clothes, using bicycles for commuting, chores, and other daily purposes. We know of Brooklyn dads and moms pedaling around New York's hippest borough, their kids in protective seats and baskets laden with groceries. We see laptop-toting tech workers with their messenger bags hanging securely around their shoulders as they move swiftly up Los Angeles's Sunset Boulevard, along with small groups of day workers on Huffys, Schwinns, and fixed-gear bikes.

We know of urban bike companies sprouting along the West Coast and more established firms manufacturing bikes and marketing others for the same consumers. These are more upright, comfortable bikes with straight handlebars. Some have old-style springs under the saddle. They look like bikes from the 1950s, or that you could find on a European street corner.

Several cities have added riders in droves. According to a recent American Community Survey, more than 6 percent of Portland, Oregon, commuters cycle to work. Portland is one of just three cities to earn Platinum status, the highest awarded, in the League of American Bicyclists' bike-friendly city survey. Portland has nearly 300 miles of bike lanes and a program to equip low-income residents with bicycles and equipment. The university towns of Davis, California, and Boulder, Colorado, are the other two platinum towns, although both have populations of less than 100,000. About one in five Davis residents commutes by bike. Portland's population is more than 500,000.

Among other larger towns such as Seattle, Tucson, and Minneapolis, cyclists now make up more than 2 percent of commuters. These numbers may not overwhelm you. But they have risen in recent years. They are signs of progress among cycling advocates.

Some movements are movements before anyone realizes it.

We see more bike lanes, parking racks, and push-out bus shelves for far-away commuters who combine public transportation and cycling for longer treks to the office. We see more co-ops and other organizations for helping the poor get on a bicycle. These groups survive largely on private donations. People support them because they believe in the transformative ability of the bicycle. Having a bike has enabled individuals to keep jobs. As little as a decade ago, there were few, if any, co-ops.

In Los Angeles and New York, we walked into two stores— Metropolis and Adeline Adeline—that focused on upright city bikes. Most had only three to eight gears. They were built not for speed but rather usefulness. There are more accessories for these old-style bikes—retro baskets, bells, and even fenders. A few helmet companies are creating products that look like traditional headwear—beanie designs, helmets with brims, helmets meant to look like riding, and gentlemen's and ladies' caps.

America's cities are nowhere near Europe's major metropolitan areas for bike friendliness. Holland's 16.5 million citizens own 18 million bicycles. They ride on nearly 30,000 kilometers—or more than 18,000 miles—of cycling lanes, which if straightened and extended around the globe east to west, would take you across the Atlantic, Pacific, and into China. Three in five Dutch citizens cycle at least three times weekly. Amsterdam residents own roughly 550,000 bikes but only about 215,000 cars. And the Danes, particularly Copenhagen, may be just as bike crazy. Daily traffic on some Copenhagen bike lanes reaches 30,000 cyclists.

You can still travel miles in many U.S. cities without seeing cyclists. But the pockets of growth give us hope that we are in the beginning stages of a movement. This movement could have enormous benefits. The Texas Transportation Institute's most recent annual study on traffic delays found that commuters stuck in congestion burned nearly 4 billion gallons of fuel at a cost of more than $12.5 billion, based on a rough estimate of current gas prices. Yet according to a 1995 National Transportation Survey, one in two people live within five miles of their jobs. That's easy cycling distance and a quick way to cut a household budget.

We drive because we're used to doing it.

Cycling burns calories, but it doesn't seem like exercise. You don't have to make an effort to get on a bike the way you do to go to a health club. Given the current epidemic of obesity—one in three people are obese in the U.S.—it would be an understatement to say that we need people to become more active. Cycling helps create tighter communities. It's easy to meet people cycling. We see this in the rise of formal and semiformal riding groups. Some meet in the wee hours when streets are emptier and more cycling friendly. We see this in the way some people smile at cyclists. Does anyone ever smile at a passing Dodge Caravan, or even a Toyota Prius?

Cycling allows both the rider and the spectator to take stock of each other and of the world. Despite the steps forward, drivers hold sway in the political arena. The cycling lobby is small and scattered. This will take a while to change.

Still, longtime bicycle industry analyst Jay Townley, among others, sees hope in the pockets of urban growth. He believes more people will be returning to cities from suburbs. He sees cycling as the most logical means of transportation for these more densely populated areas. Townley is a former Schwinn executive who has spent more than four decades working in the cycling industry. His Gluskin-Townley Group publishes an annual report on sales. Partly because of the number of retailers in cities, he believes that urban cycling has established a "beachhead" in bike-friendly cities. He is optimistic about future growth. "It's going to grow," he said. "There are already more bike-friendly cities. By 2020, a movement will be more established. Baby boomers have already wanted to go back to the bike. The country isn't going back to the days of Detroit. It's going forward."

Ride on.

—*James Rubin*

Am I up for The Challenge again, today?

That's all that goes through my mind as I reluctantly wake up to the sound of my CD alarm clock.

My dog's only reaction to our CD wake-up call was to roll onto her back, arching her body into a question mark, her legs bent up like the appendages of a dead cockroach, her face begging for a belly rub: "Mornings be damned," Ziggy's eyes emoted, "rub my belly!"

So I did. While Ziggy's eyes peacefully closed, mine involuntarily blinked open, reluctantly, like I was breaking in new eyelids. Instinctively, I scanned the skies for dark clouds, paying attention to the wind to see if it was coming from the north, the one sure sign in the Midwest of bad weather. No heavy rains or winds meant no excuses for not riding.

Some days, I must admit I'm happy to wake up to monsoon-like conditions, and the decision whether or not to ride is all but made for me (unless I think I can wait out the worst and ride in the storm's wake). Years ago, I considered waking up to an ice storm, flash flood, or knee-deep snow storm to be an omen of impending doom. I'd go into the day waiting for the next shoe to drop when in fact nothing horrible had happened. Now I view Mother Nature's hissy fits as nothing more than the perfect excuse to not ride.

Those days are rare, however, because even on the bad days I still convince myself to accept The Challenge.

A few minutes later, I'm still stumbling toward consciousness, being dragged behind Ziggy who is sniffing her way from puddle to stain along the dirty sidewalk.

Was it Monday already? Did I need to eat all that pizza during the game yesterday? Why is my knee so sore? How could Virginia Tech blow another lead? Oh, man, I think I have that conference call this morning! Wouldn't it be easier to just take the train? Is it going to rain? How's the wind today? Take the bus? What's wrong with my ankle, why's it so stiff? Wonder if it'll rain this week....

The Challenge is always the same: "Are you cycling today?"

Excuses cascade over the floodwall of my mind: bad knee, rotten ankle, sore shoulder.

Alternatives make themselves available: take the train, ride the bus, hail a cab.

When I started riding daily in 2004, The Challenge was closer to a 50-50 guess. I was quicker to take the urine-scented train or cram myself into the smell-your-neighbor bus than I was to cycle to work.

But by the start of 2005 I had found my groove and was riding easily more than 200 days per year. It was easier to count the days I didn't ride than the ones I did.

All I need to do is think of the annoyance at watching three or four buses—always the same route, of course—go past your bus stop before your bus pulls to the curb, overstuffed with equally annoyed riders, and the temptation to avoid The Challenge diminishes. The negatives to taking mass transit nearly always sway my wishy-washy, early morning mind toward the open-air option of the bicycle.

I ignore the fact that I'll gladly pick up Ziggy's poop early in the morning, but the thought of smelling another human's urine makes me gag even thinking about it.

My commute from Wrigleyville to Printer's Row in Chicago is six miles. Both the bus and the train take at least 45 minutes to cover the distance, and that doesn't include waiting on the platform or through a parade of buses. I cover the same distance in 30 minutes or less each day. That simple math always convinces the lazy part of my mind to give in whenever The Challenge is raised in my head.

Forty minutes later, showered, changed, my clothes packed in a pannier, and Ziggy chowing on breakfast, I head into work wondering why I still keep riding each morning. Why do I constantly feel the need to meet The Challenge that is simply an artificial construct in my mind? I ride and think about the "why" of cycling, but three blocks later I'm forced to address the real world.

The entire block north of Addison St.—the street that houses my famous neighbor, Wrigley Field—is being resurfaced. I note that it's been that way for two weeks now, and I can't help but notice that other streets in my neighborhood are in worse condition. Other sections of Wrigleyville have been paved too, I'm forced to admit, and without expecting it, I'm just this much less annoyed with my local alderman, another unexpected positive outcome of cycling. In fact, I noticed just a couple months earlier that Clark St.—one of the main north-south pathways in the city and the main route of my daily ride—had large sections of the street repaved. I told myself to send a note of thanks to city hall, but somehow have let that slip. I'm reminded of these things, too.

There's barely any time to enjoy the short stretch of smooth ride before I'm slowing instinctively. The worst enemy a city cyclist can have is approaching quickly: coffee shops. Java-chasing motorists infamously pull their vehicle as close to the curb as their caffeine withdrawal will allow before throwing open their car door and spinning blindly out of their driver's seat in pursuit of a venti. How many accidents and near collisions at this one coffee shop alone? I slow down, my eyes scanning each rearview mirror for the quick flash of jewelry, fingernails, teeth, or reflection from glasses that reveal a motorist preparing to bound into traffic.

My mind flashes momentarily to the conference call later that morning and the second one scheduled for that afternoon before I notice a panel truck turning into traffic in front of me, bringing me close enough to the truck's passenger to see the doughnut goo between his teeth. Suddenly I feel more awake than any jolt of java could give me. I pump my legs twice, and in less than two seconds I'm 30' in front of the truck, through the intersection, and have "squeezed off" the panel truck, which idles back at the intersection halted by a red light.

My speed is greater now, potholes coming faster as I lean left, right, and left again to avoid what I can. The ones that I can't avoid I have to jump. Taking a pothole at 15 mph isn't a good idea if you want to arrive at work with all your blood still in your veins.

My blood is pumping quickly now. I'm breathing heavier, and all thoughts of aldermen and conference calls are as far from my mind as possible. I no longer even notice the soreness in my knee or the stiffness of my surgically repaired ankle. Buses leapfrog each other while a garbage truck juts its stinky nose into traffic daring anyone to touch it. I keep scanning rearview mirrors for movement while watching for potholes, street cracks, and pedestrians cutting between parked cars while maintaining safe speed and distance from other vehicles.

But that's not all that runs through my mind. There are buses, too.

I pass Crossroads Tavern and see the familiar Virginia Tech flags in the window. I remember the Hokies' loss from this past weekend and get seismically angry all over again. However, I instantly see the sign for Weiner Circle, an infamous after-hours hangout for good greasy food at 2:00 AM. To me it's infamous all right, but not for culinary reasons. No, I know the bus stop in front of Weiner Circle is popular, which means there is always a bus coming. Sure enough, as I turn to look for the next bus squeezing down Clark Street, I feel the wall-like shadow of the bus fall over my shoulder. The bus rearview mirror hovers inches from my helmet. My egg-beater legs pump into a blur as I go over 20 mph, and I'm through the intersection, past the traffic, and all the lights go yellow as I pass through the intersection.

At Clark and LaSalle I'm forced to stop my bike for the first time in more than three miles. As I catch my breath, three more cyclists pull up next to me. One guy has flip-flops on, audio ear buds in his ears, and no helmet. I instantly hope that natural selection will weed him out today, but say nothing. There are two other cyclists coagulating behind me—neither wearing a helmet; one has on headphones.

Back in 2004, I had days when I never even saw another cyclist. Seriously—entire days when I didn't see a cyclist. Granted, those were winter days when snow and ice made cycling dangerous (a risk I, my doctors, and surgeon no longer endorse). However, by 2010 the number of cyclists had noticeably increased. A cyclist cannot help but notice that within a few years the amount of bicycle traffic at stoplights went from nonexistent to panting in a wolf pack at each light jockeying for position.

When the light goes green, I blast past the novices to establish position on the other side of the intersection where wide trucks driving past parked cars can leave too narrow an alley to ride through if you aren't aggressive enough to establish position first. I hear honking behind me directed at one of the cyclists in my wake. I glance back to see the cyclist weaving back and forth as he tries to control the handlebars while starting from a stop, and I think how I can't blame the traffic for honking the way it is. At the very least, this cyclist isn't even strong enough to control his handlebars and acceleration, much less making himself a danger by wearing ear buds while riding.

I squeeze off the three cyclists at the next intersection. Normally I can relax at this point, coasting through the Gold Coast. However, I remember the bike messenger who leveled me a couple years ago when he was riding through here, and I tense up. He came out of nowhere, going the wrong way on a one-way street and plowed into me like a black rhino sending me ass over ears, flipping my bike.

That accident taught me as much as face-planting on the trunk of a taxi cab or the 5'4" female jogger who caused permanent scars on my hands and shoulder or a dog who cracked my helmet or the teenager who doored me with her Honda or... well, you get the idea. There's something to learn from every accident, which means I've had plenty of opportunities to learn.

In the Loop, I decide that traffic is getting too thick, and I want to park my bike as soon as possible. Without pausing, I crank my pedaling into a high gear going from 15 mph to 25 mph in a 50' span. I pass a couple of buses and start passing more traffic until I reach the Chicago River. At that point the only thing I'm reading are the pedestrians scurrying to work. At this time of the day, crosswalks mean very little. Pedestrians are in the middle of the street, crossing against the light, walking wherever they like. The theory in the Loop is basically this: go ahead and hit me, I can use the insurance money.

In a way, I share that mentality, too. Not that I want to get hit, but I have been. In fact, I've been hit by every kind of vehicle and nonvehicle there is, and every single time I've gotten back on my bike. Why? Because that's part of The Challenge.

The Challenge is as much about shaving my commute time in half as it is about spending a mere fraction on my transportation as noncyclists do. The Challenge is as much about giving myself the freedom to go anywhere I want, whenever I want despite owning no gas-burning vehicle. The Challenge is as much about doing whatever a car owner can do without owning a car, paying insurance, or fussing over broken engines. The Challenge has become about more in recent years as more novice cyclists take to the roads. The Challenge is now as much about leading by example as it is getting home from work quicker than any bus or train or car could carry me. The Challenge now is mostly about helping all the new cyclists on the roads, showing them how they can ride smarter and be safer.

More than 200 times per year for at least six years I have met The Challenge, and what has come of it? A few scars and a couple scary moments for sure. But also the knowledge that in the worst of moments I've kept my cool, prevailed, and even if medical assistance has been needed, I've been perfectly fine afterward.

I'm not superhuman. I'm overweight and lazy and would prefer to hang out at a bar with friends than to log a century on my bike. If I can easily incorporate cycling into my daily routine, anybody can.

While I'm locking up my bike, I remember my conference calls and the research work I have planned for the day. Before I get into the elevator I start to smile, realizing that I've planned my morning out between red lights without realizing it. Three other people are in the elevator with me, two of them yawning and the third somnambulant rubbing her eyes awake. But I'm fully awake, sweating even, and my day is already planned out. The work stress I felt earlier is gone, sweated out on my ride.

Relaxed, awake, and energized by my 30-minute ride between trucks and cars, I'm ready to start the day thanks to my ride.

However, I can't help but think about all the cyclists on the streets today without helmets, wearing flip-flops and ear buds. I think of the cyclist who was killed last month downtown and the other cyclist seriously injured on the Southside last week.

As I sit down to my desk I know that I've met The Challenge and have improved my survival rate over the years thanks to what I've learned.

But what about Mr. Flip-Flops or Miss Ear Buds? Their actions are not just irresponsible for their own safety. By breaking nearly all the rules of the road, they simply make things worse for other safe cyclists because they have made other motorists angry at cyclists for very good reasons. If I ride next to a motorist who has had a bad experience with a cyclist lately, the motorist is going to take it out on me, not the memory he has.

So this book is written for Mr. Flip-Flops and Miss Ear Buds.
—*Scott Rowan*

Acknowledgments

I would like to thank my wife, Chris, for her encouragement and suggestions. I know of no better journalist—or partner. My thanks to my son Harper for being a good sport on our ride to school, to my daughter Saskia for her usual good cheer and art work, and my parents Cyrus and Mary Ellen, who encouraged my curiosities and interest in sports. Triumph's Noah Amstadter was a thoughtful and patient editor. Scott Rowan's enthusiasm for urban cycling and the *Urban Cyclist's Survival Guide* was contagious. He is a true city rider. Tom Bast of Triumph Books brought me into the project and introduced me to Scott. Thank you to Triumph for sensing a trend and embracing a cycling book. I'd like to thank the many cyclists, mechanics, advocates, and enthusiasts around the country who were generous with their time and expertise. But special thanks are in order for Larry Hoffman, who not only answered all my questions, but served as a model for our photographs on safe riding. Kelly Martin and the ever-kind Jonathan West allowed me to tag along on their commutes and shared their insights on city cycling. A special thanks to T.J. Flexer and Ace Carretero of Orange Cycle 20, a rocking bike shop if ever there was one. T.J. let us spend hours photographing bikes and accessories. Ace was of great help in discussing helmet and bike fitting. Thank you also to Julie Hirschfeld of New York's Adeline Adeline and Diego Souza and the folks at Los Angeles's Safety Cycle for their thoughts respectively on bike accessories and maintenance. If my recent travels in those two cities are any indication, there will be many more cyclists on city streets in coming years. Mark Halliday was enormously helpful in discussing cycling attire, particularly for cold, wet weather. A final thanks to Michal Czerwonka and Jonathan Maus for their exceptional photographs, and to the Bicycle Museum of America for providing pictures of historic bicycles and their forerunners.

— *James Rubin*

I'd like to thank all the friends, colleagues, and professionals who helped our research while writing this book including Dr. Tim Roberts, Dr. Leon James, Bill Jackson, Tim Mollette-Parks, Mike Zinski, Scott Andresen, Gerald Rowan, Bryan Finigan, Julian Sayerer, Joy Miles, Dave Bunce, Colby Marple, Christina Curas, Carrie Cizauskas, Eric Anderson, Amy Snyder, Eric Bjorling, John A. Lewert, and Tom White. I also want to personally thank everyone at Triumph Books who helped in all phases of the publishing process including Mitch Rogatz, Tom Bast, Noah Amstadter, Mark Bast, and Don Gulbrandsen. But my biggest gratitude and eternal thanks goes to the one female who has been with me through the good and bad times and always made me want to arrive home safely after every ride so we could go chase squirrels in the park—Ziggy, the cutest dog in the world.

— *Scott Rowan*

THE
Urban Cyclist's
SURVIVAL GUIDE

1

History

Velocipedes, Bone-Crushers, High-Wheelers,
Safety Cycles...and Schwinns

We have a nonsecret.

An urban cyclist doesn't need to know about bicycle history. Knowledge of velocipedes, also called draisines; boneshakers, so-called for the jarring ride of their tire-less wheels; the high-wheelers, so-called for their monumental, circus-like front wheels; and safety cycles—let alone American Wheelmen, Schwinns, Raleighs, Campagnolo derailleurs, hybrids, double-shocked mountain bikes, and high-tech carbon frames—won't guide your lock and helmet selection, take you safely around corners, or help plot commuting routes through Washington, D.C. Do we care which innovation preceded another?

Exit our inner curmudgeon. We think of the writer George Santayana, who was big on history. He said, "A country without memory is a country of madmen." We don't like the idea that someone might consider us crazy, although a few automobile drivers have said as much as they've passed us on narrow roads.

In the words of our elementary school teachers, take out your notebooks.

Famous People on Bikes

Bicycling history is rich. It spans at least a half-dozen wars. Indeed, the oft-anointed father of the American cycling industry, Albert Pope, wanted to make cycles an integral part of the army. Cycles were used in training toward the end of the nineteenth century and by troops in World War I, for transport, not charging the enemy. Civilian usage boomed during both world wars as countries diverted scarce metal and steel to weaponry and motor vehicles. Cycling history touches many famous people. The poet John Keats wrote disdainfully about early bikes. Mark Twain penned—and *penned* was an apt word at the time—an essay about trying to ride a bicycle. It was funny.

President Woodrow Wilson enjoyed cycling, but probably not with the top hat he donned in public. In an oft-told tale, recounted in David Herlihy's excellent history, *Bicycle*, Wilson's presidential car nailed a young cyclist. Wilson asked his physician to check on the boy and presented him with a new bicycle in the hospital. "I did not know it was the president's car that I ran into," the boy said. Wilson responded, "I rather thought it was the president's car that ran into you." Would that modern drivers followed the Wilson model.

Ike liked bikes, or at least Dwight Eisenhower's doctor instructed him to ride one after he suffered a heart attack. Jimmy Carter, Bill Clinton, and George W. Bush rode bikes while in office. W's dedication to mountain biking was a sore point with critics who felt he had his priorities wrong. On the other hand, it kept him busy.

Movie stars bicycled. In the golden age of Hollywood, studios kept bicycles on the set for actors. *Philadelphia Inquirer* movie critic Stephen Rea recently launched a blog with photos of cycling entertainers. The pictures include the rugged Western star Glen Ford riding at Paramount with Rita Hayworth nestled on the top tube, legs dangling to the side; Clark Gable wearing adventure boots and a neckerchief; and Robin Hood himself, Errol Flynn, straddling back-lot bikes. Moving forward in time, we see a young, bicycling Elvis; an

Actor Humphrey Bogart and his wife, actress Lauren Bacall, ride bicycles in 1948 while on the Hollywood set of the film *Key Largo*. (KM ARCHIVE/GETTY IMAGES)

even younger Julie Christie on an early fold-up cycle; Audrey Hepburn with her yorkie, Mr. Famous, in a whicker basket; James Dean; Sean Connery; and Bill Murray. Except for the serious Flynn, they all look quite satisfied with themselves.

One of the most famous pictures of a cyclist shows Albert Einstein beaming as he rides at a friend's house in Santa Barbara. The twentieth century's greatest genius wears the unlikely cycling outfit of tweed pants, sensible shoes, a cardigan, and thin tie. The utilitarian frame with handlebars curling like longhorns is clearly too small. He can't extend his legs when the pedal has reached its nadir. Einstein's famous wild hair is swept back. His eyes crinkle "fun" as he turns left from the strong California sun.

Bah to cycling history, you say? Such pictures remind us of cycling's inherent joyousness. Indeed, we defy you to find a cyclist—famous or otherwise—who doesn't look happy.

Cycling economics have enough ups and downs for a Six Flags roller coaster. Bike sales skyrocketed in the Great Depression, the oil embargo of the 1970s, and the most recent recession. During these periods, people had to cut corners and return to the simple life. It meant survival with a capital S, and bicycles were an important part. The great movie maker Vittorio de Sica speaks to this necessity in his masterpiece *Bicycle Thieves*, which takes place in post–World War II Italy. The country's economy has been demoralized, and a scruffy, old bike represents the hero's only opportunity to commute to his job. When thieves steal it, he sees his hopes of feeding his family vanish, and he spends most of the story trying to retrieve it. In the end, he contemplates stealing a replacement bike.

It's a dreary story that resonates loudly today as an increasing number of low-wage workers, many of them immigrants, rely on bicycles to carry them to scarce jobs. They cannot afford automobiles—or $4.00-per-gallon gas. So many of them are recycling bicycles from Goodwill shops, thrift stores, and yes, garbage heaps. "There's a perception that people turn to bikes out of economic necessity," said Arlen Jones, a founder of la Bici Digna, a Los Angeles organization that provides bikes and related resources for low-income workers. "It's a dignified transportation alternative."

Bike usage dropped when the automobile arrived and during flush times when people didn't think they had to worry about the environment, budgets, or getting back to basics.

But mostly, the bicycle shows man's remarkable ability, when fully engaged in a problem, to progress rapidly from concept to finished product. Think of it. Man spent more than a million years getting around by walking and riding horses, oxcarts, and elephants.

Then, in less than a half century, he had a self-generating means of transportation that could match the speed of a steam locomotive for short distances and cover huge swathes of territory via paved roads. By the 1860s, cyclists were already riding tens of miles in a single day. One of these events is considered a precursor to the Tour de France. All of this happened without panniers, Starbucks, carbon forks, or Michelin guides.

The evolution of the bicycle demonstrates the growing speed with which people could share ideas and build on each other's work. Much of this took place in cities whose populations grew rapidly as methods of mass production improved and factories sprouted, including those for bicycles. Albert Pope saw the potential for bicycles and began mass-producing high-wheelers in the late 1870s. A few years later, he helped found the League of American Wheelman, now the Washington, D.C.–based advocacy group known as the League of American

Bicyclists. He was also one of the ringleaders of the Good Roads movement that began paving thoroughfares. By the time the latter movement kick-started, Pope was manufacturing the more user-friendly safety cycle or low-mount, named for the lower positioning of the seat. In the mid-1890s, at the peak of the first great bicycle boom, the Pope Manufacturing Company employed more than 2,000 people, and his factory floor covered 17 acres.

Pope honed the work of the people before him. Early lines of bicycle invention were not always so clear. Its development combined the brainpower of smart, technologically savvy people working on the same problems independently, separated by great distances. Many lived in cities where ideas flowed readily, and large audiences could ogle the latest devices and spread the news. If you were strolling Paris's Bois de Boulogne in the last three decades of the nineteenth century, boater or bonnet beclad, it would not have been unusual to see some version of a cyclist making the rounds. We consider these muscled, mustachioed cyclists the first urban cyclists.

In the Beginning

The most surprising aspect of bike history is its brevity. You'd think in a world that invented the wheel three or four millennia or so before the Roman chariot, that the bicycle would have followed immediately. Surely, a flat, two-wheeled machine with a connecting chain wouldn't represent such a big departure from the two- and four-wheeled carriages that carried Caesars past adoring mobs. Or surely Marco Polo would have imported chain power from the Far East, along with gun powder and pasta. Or that Leonardo would have sketched the first prototype along with his drawings of flying machines. Or what about some great thinker from the Enlightenment? A king? A

The draisine, an early 1800s predecessor to the bicycle, lacked a key ingredient—pedals. (BICYCLE MUSEUM OF AMERICA)

queen? Isaac Newton? Galileo? Benjamin Franklin seeking a transportation alternative when his gout erupted?

None of the above.

The bicycle isn't much older than the telegraph, telephone, sewing machine, photograph, electric light, or zipper, iconic inventions of the nineteenth-century Victorian era. The bike's forerunner appears less than two centuries ago, courtesy of assorted inventors working in different parts of Europe. They included Karl von Drais, a Baden (Germany) baron who grew fascinated by the possibility of a horseless carriage. David Herlihy speculates that Drais was looking for a faster way to monitor the huge forest lands surrounding his estate in southwest Germany.

Drais invented a four-wheel, hand-crank-powered vehicle before he created his bike forerunner. The draisine, or velocipede from the Latin word for fast foot, was sleek by nineteenth-century standards, had cushioning for royal behinds, and on good roads with favorable tailwinds, could match the speed of a slow horse. It also probably enhanced the nobleman's all-important quotient of dashing-ness as he blazed through pastoral parks, wool coattails flying. Velocipedes created a stir in Paris, Vienna, Manheim, Frankfurt, and other European cities. Some saw them as a future wave, easily accessible personal transportation that was not dependent on four hooves. Others saw them as a threat to public safety.

But the velocipede lacked one set of key ingredients: pedals. Neither Drais nor anyone else around 1820 had imagined a rear-wheel chain drive or other systems allowing riders to move without touching ground. Think of the draisine and imagine your little nephew straddling a preschool, pedal-less bike and pushing off Fred Flintstone style. For its time, the draisine was clearly clever and hip. But a rider could only coast for so long, and it clearly wasn't much for rough roads or hills. After a brief period of curiosity—and disdain in some parts—the velocipede receded from serious public consciousness.

Who invented the pedal-driven bicycle nearly a half century after the first Draisine is a subject of some mystery, if not controversy. Let's start with what's clear. There were a bunch of Frenchmen involved. They seemed to argue a lot with each other and other people. The first prototype appeared in the 1860s. It had front-wheel drive and all the comfort of a moving cast iron pipe. The public was cautiously interested in what some referred to as a mechanical horse.

Here's the mystery. Most people credited Pierre Michaux for introducing the first bicycle. Pierre was a Parisian blacksmith and a perfectly good candidate for inventor. He worked with iron. He knew about bikes in the mid-1860s. He seemed to be the first person to sell bikes on a wider basis. But Herlihy makes a convincing case that Pierre Lallement is the more likely culprit. Lallement, a craftsman of children's perambulators and tricycles who bore a passing resemblance to Agatha

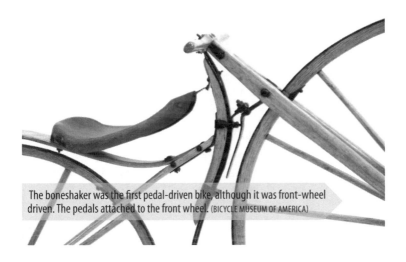

The boneshaker was the first pedal-driven bike, although it was front-wheel driven. The pedals attached to the front wheel. (BICYCLE MUSEUM OF AMERICA)

Christie's detective Hercules Poirot, had knowledge. There's evidence that Lallement had already invented a front-wheel-drive cycle by the early 1860s.

High-Wheelers and Safety Cycles

In the ensuing years, entrepreneurial types and inventors tinkered with the design. By the late 1870s, high-wheel bikes, also called Penny Farthings, were in vogue. Penny Farthings draw their name from the penny and the farthing, a much larger coin. Observers liken the disparity in wheel size to the difference in coin size. High-wheelers were one of those cartoonish developments that seems progressive at the time. The big wheel would generate more speed. (These days, high-wheelers would have their advantages for seeing over SUVs.)

But the 40" and 50" front wheels weren't much for balance or safety, let alone ease in dismounting. The popularity of high-wheelers was already waning by the end of the following decade with the introduction of low-mount, rear-drive machines. So-called safety cycles incorporated chains to connect pedaling

Why Wet Roads Are Bad

City cyclists should learn what NASCAR drivers already know—slick tires are your friend.

When it comes to bicycle tires, it's all about surface area: the more contact your bicycle tire has with city streets, the safer you are.

Bridges, manhole covers, construction covers, and any kind of smooth metal on the road surface can quickly become a dangerous impediment to the average urban cyclist when weather conditions get wet. It doesn't matter if it's rain, sleet, or melting snow, any precipitation can easily cause an accident. Why? It turns out that Mother Nature's slick conditions are trickier than they appear and present problems that no technology has fully countered.

When bicycles first appeared in the 1800s, wheels were wooden with metal "tires" wrapped around them to prevent deterioration. That made for jarring, jolting rides. In the late 1880s, John Dunlop was credited with inventing the first modern tire by wrapping his son's bicycle wheels in rubber to reduce the pounding the rider experienced.

Rubber has been and is still used today because it provides a smooth ride, is resistant to wearing down, and is flexible enough to conform to irregularities in the surface. It maintains contact with the ground. Gripping qualities have little (if anything) to do with rubber being the worldwide default material used in tires. In fact, additives like silicon and butyl rubber *reduce* traction in favor of longer tire life. Grooves, knobs, and channels are added to tires to transfer as much water out from between the tire and the road as possible in order to increase the amount of contact between the tire and the road. That is why NASCAR drivers use smooth tires that have no knobs or channels—to increase the surface area their tires have with the track. Rubber does not inherently grip the road. It creates traction by giving the bike a solid connection to the ground.

City cyclists should use tires that have no knobs but instead have channels that allow water to be moved while maintaining as much contact with the surface as possible.

It has been approximately 150 years since tires and wheels became part of everyday life, and humans have yet to find a material that truly grips the road in an advanced way. The best we have come up with is increasing contact surface area, improving flexibility of the tire (to further increase surface area) while making the tire as resistant to punctures as possible.

The American Safety, sometimes called a high-wheeler or penny farthing, was popular in the 1870s and 80s. (BICYCLE MUSEUM OF AMERICA)

mechanisms to the rear wheel. But their real advantage came with the development of the same double-diamond frame design you'll find today and rubber tires with inner tubes filled with compressed air. The latter innovation introduced by the Scottish veterinarian John Dunlop cushioned the ride to unparalleled levels. The improvements made bicycling more enjoyable and popular. Factories benefiting from easier access to raw materials and technological advancements had no difficulty meeting demand.

Wax your moustache and ride downtown to watch the great Cy Young pitch a few innings in the nascent professional baseball league, or hear Enrico Caruso sing a few bars. It was boom time for bicycles. Indeed, the bike was the perfect symbol for the roaring '90s, a period of technological, cultural, and social change. Bikes were fun, looked cool, and enabled the average person to get where he wanted without the expenses of keeping a horse.

Racing

We'd be remiss not to mention the bicycle's place in society's eternal quest to go faster. By this time, we'd pretty much seen the limits of the horse. Earlier versions of the bicycle had raced frequently with success against horses. As bikes improved, their potential seemed huge. By the mid-1890s, bike races were among the world's biggest sporting events. Six-day races at New York's famed Madison Square Garden matched riders from the U.S., Australia, and Europe and drew tens of thousands of people. The leading riders covered more than 1,500 miles. Other races in major urban centers—Brooklyn, Boston, Indianapolis, Philadelphia—saw riders compete against each other or the clock at distances ranging from long sprints to the mile and eventually against steam-powered vehicles. But while the quest for speed stimulated interest, it also led to the boom's end. Cars could go faster and along with airplanes replaced bikes in the public fascination.

The Bicycle Finds Itself

Once bicycle inventors got things right, they got it right. Subsequent changes to the bicycle have involved refinement more than a drastic overhaul. In the early decades of the twentieth century, they included a removable rear freewheel that would allow riders to engage in the wonderfully freeing exercise of coasting on your pedals, and caliper brakes to stop more easily and efficiently.

The Black Phantom was introduced by Schwinn in 1949 and was popular in the ensuing decade. Schwinn patented the cantilever design. Note the fat tires and chrome plating.

Early caliper brakes resembled those used today, pinching the wheel just below the tire. This period saw the creation of spring-supported seats, fenders, and more water-resistant materials. Brooks introduced its first leather seats. Its latest versions are still considered among the biking world's best. Another English company introduced the first three-speed internal hub with gears for climbing hills. The internal hub—usually three or eight gears—has made a small renaissance in recent years as sales of old-style, city cycles have grown. Other companies honed the external derailleur, which enabled companies to offer bicycles with 28 gears. We cannot use many of these gears.

Everyone worked on making bikes lighter. Some early twentieth-century models weighed more than 50 pounds, and that was without laptops. Try pedaling that up Telegraph Hill in San Francisco or the Boyle Heights neighborhood in Los Angeles. And we would be remiss not to tip our helmets to the Italian manufacturer Tullio Campagnolo, who, legend has it, suffered a flat tire and was frustrated by the amount of time it took to remove the wheel. Campagnolo, whose name is now synonymous with super-light, high-end racing cycles,

Most Expensive Bike in the World

Apparently half a million dollars doesn't buy what it used to. In November 2009, the Trek Madone Butterfly bike, created specifically for Lance Armstrong's second comeback to the Tour de France, sold at a Sotheby's auction to an undisclosed buyer. If you are new to the planet, Armstrong was the first cyclist to win the Tour de France seven consecutive years, his streak ending after the 2005 race when he retired from professional cycling. However, by 2009 Armstrong wanted to compete again in the world-famous race. Discussion among Nike CEO Mark Parker, Trek, and Armstrong's foundation, Livestrong, hatched an idea to blend sports and art to raise funds to fight cancer. The result: seven artists around the world were given a Trek Madone bicycle (the company's premier mass-production bicycle that normally sells for $4,000 to $5,000) as a blank canvas.

Enter controversial artist Damien Hirst, who was atop the short list of artists that Parker and Armstrong wanted to work with on what became known as the Stages project. Considered Britain's wealthiest artist, Hirst is famous for pieces that push boundaries of accepted art and focus on life and death. While many may argue the artistic value of his most (in)famous pieces of art like *The Golden Calf* (a bull calf covered in gold and preserved in formaldehyde) or *The Physical Impossibility of Death in the Mind of Someone Living* (a 17' display of a tiger shark preserved in formaldehyde), they cannot deny that Hirst's art sells. In 2008, *The Golden*

Lance Armstrong rode the Madone Butterfly, a bicycle created by artist Damien Hirst using the wings of real butterflies. (AP IMAGES)

Calf sold for a record-setting $18.5 million, topping Hirst's previous "high-water" mark of $17 million for *The Physical Impossibility of Death in the Mind of Someone Living*, also sold in 2008.

What vision did a death-obsessed artist have for a Lance Armstrong bike? He removed the wings from real butterflies to decorate the bike.

"I wanted to use real butterflies and not just pictures of butterflies, because I wanted it to shimmer when the light catches it like only real butterflies do," Hirst explained in promotional materials at the auction.

Armstrong rode the Madone Butterfly down the Champs Elysées during the 2009 Tour's final stage, and in November 2009 that bike and six others that Armstrong used during the season were auctioned for a total of $1.25 million.

Before anyone starts thinking up picket sign slogans, Trek media relations spokesman Erik Bjorling cautions against potential outrage. "All of the butterflies that were used on the bike were harvested naturally and allowed to live out their complete lives before becoming immortalized on one of the world's most remarkable bicycles," Bjorling said. "Absolutely no butterflies were killed expressly for this project. What Hirst did was take something exquisitely beautiful from the natural world and allow it to live another noble life in the form of a piece of work that was done for charity."

Where is the bike today? Only the anonymous buyer knows.

"The bike was purchased privately and currently resides in somebody's personal collection," Bjorling said. "Seeing as the bike was done by Hirst and ridden down the Champs Elysées by Lance, I doubt it's ever touched the pavement since."

invented a quick-release skewer. The mechanism has brightened the lives of many urban cyclists faced with in-transit tire repairs. Molti Grazie.

Bicycle design altered little through all these changes and adornments. Handlebars curved slightly. Riders sat upright. American models were heavier and clunkier—balloon tires were popular through the middle of the century—than most brands from Europe, where ridership soared after the Second World War. Participation in the U.S. waned in the 1950s amidst a deluge of suburbs, road building, and automobiles, except among children who, Norman Rockwell–style, rode to school on their Schwinns. The Schwinn name comes from Ignaz Schwinn, a midwestern entrepreneur who founded the company in 1895. In the 1960s, Schwinns helped fuel a mini-surge in the U.S. with their Sting-Rays. The post–baby boom generation remembers them for their bright colors, longhorn handlebars, and banana split seats that looked like lounge chairs compared to the usual saddle.

Lighter ten-speed models from Europe, and a few years later from Japan, spurred another spike in bicycle participation, although much of it occurred outside cities, where bike lanes and cyclists had about the same status as stray cats. A burgeoning interest in off-road riding in the late 1970s and early 1980s sparked the creation of mountain bikes with thick, stubby tires, shocks, and straight handlebars. The tires drew their inspiration from balloon tires of earlier decades. Mountain bikes would prove better suited for scarred, urban streets than the most expensive road bikes crafted of space-age carbon fiber and titanium. They would spawn a generation of hybrids that combined an upright ride with smoother, thinner tires.

Meanwhile, over the past three decades, the cycling climate has improved.

It was the efforts of a few determined advocates and government officials in the 1970s that began changing the national climate for cyclists. In 1980, Washington, D.C., attorney and cycling enthusiast Tedson Meyers created the first national trade group focused on bicycle advocacy. The Intermodal Surface Transportation Efficiency Act a decade later funneled unprecedented funding to state bicycling projects. A subsequent survey released by the Department of Transportation recommended increasing bikeways and safety programs to help convince people to use bicycles more. These events dovetailed with a revival of many downtowns. Bicycles were perfect for getting around in a low-cost, environmentally kind way.

And today?

When it comes to riding bicycles, the U.S. remains far behind Europe, most of Asia, and other parts of the world. According to the National Sporting Goods Association, just 38 million people—roughly one-ninth of the U.S. population—bicycled at least six times during 2009. In its annual survey, the League of American Bicyclists found that 0.55 percent of commuters use the bicycle. By contrast, about one-quarter of the Netherlands' population cycles. Denmark is hoping to increase the number of bicyclists to 50 percent of all commuters.

Yet the U.S. has seen pockets of improvement. In Portland, the number of bicycling commuters has roughly doubled since 2000. New York–based actor and former messenger Chris Rommelmann remembers when almost no one rode over the Brooklyn Bridge or any of the other prominent East River crossings. He traveled in regular traffic lanes and was often in fear that he would be driven down. Now cyclists and pedestrians are separated from cars, and there are ant lines in both directions. "There was almost no one on the bridge," said Rommelmann. "Now, as a cyclist, you have to dodge people."

The Brief History of the Bicycle

15000–10000 B.C. Paleolithic men used primitive tools, drew pictures on cave walls of themselves hunting animals with sticks. No evidence of bicycles or even wheels.

3500–3000 B.C. Early forbearers of Iraqi culture paint first known images of wheels on pottery. A bike would be a great idea, but no one thinks of it.

2000–1 B.C. Egyptians, Greeks, Romans create chariots. Ben Hur becomes the world's leading jockey. No bicycles.

1 A.D.–1695 People may have considered the possibility of a horseless carriage but didn't invent it. No bikes.

1696 In the journal *Recreations Mathematiques*, the French mathematician Jacques Ozanam writes of the potential of a horseless carriage complete with a drawing of a four-wheel vehicle.

1774–1804 Every few years, inventors in Europe and North America produce new versions of horseless carriages.

1813 Meet Karl von Drais. Von Drais produces his own version of a horseless carriage.

1819 The Baden Baron introduces his two-wheeled velocipede, later called a Draisine.

1819–1850s Other inventors introduce their velocipedes. But response is mixed. *How do you get that up a hill?*

1860s Now we're getting somewhere. The first bicycles to resemble the versions we know appear. Assorted Frenchmen have a big argument over who should get credit for the first pedal-powered bicycle.

1870s Early bicycles are called bone-shakers for a reason. Air-filled tires hadn't been invented. Riders rode on rims. Roads were rocky.

1880s The heyday of the high-wheel era. A big front tire made you go faster so high-wheelers became the rage among bicycle enthusiasts. *That was fun. Now how do I get off?*

1888 That feels good. The Scottish veterinarian John Dunlop invents air-filled tires.

Late 1890s–early 1900s Back to the future The safety cycle reintroduces the beauties of the low-mount, albeit this time with a chain-driven rear wheel. Bicycling becomes the "in" activity with companies sprouting all over. Thousands flock to bike racing.

Around 1900–1910 Like all fads, cycling fades. People looking for speed turn to a new invention, the car. Hill dwellers welcome the introduction of a more advanced gearing system.

1910s–30s Interest in cycling ebbs and flows. Manufacturers work streamlining designs.

1934 Tire changes made easier Tullio Campagnolo introduces the quick-release hub.

1940s–50s Cycling increases during World War II and declines in the prosperous aftermath.

1970s Introduction of the first mountain bikes.

1980s Mountain biking becomes more popular. For periods, so do racing bikes.

1990s–2000s Lance Armstrong wins seven Tours de France. Bike architecture and accessories grow increasingly sophisticated. But as the recession hits home, more people turn to hybrids and European-style city bikes with more surely to follow as gas surpasses $4 per gallon.

2

Fitness

Bicycle Riding Will Make You Healthier

We've noticed the health benefits of bicycling for years—for our friends, neighbors, family, and ourselves. But we'd like everyone in and out of cities to know them too, so they cycle more and buy lots of our books. Then we'll retire early.

And focus more on cycling.

And becoming fitter.

Health is a serious issue these days, particularly in the U.S. Many people say that Americans have become complacent, fat, and happy. We're not so sure about the happy part, but we're still seeing many rotund waistlines. When it comes to fat, the U.S. is a world leader.

We won't browbeat you with numbers but give you the latest fat analysis from the U.S. Centers for Disease Control, the go-to people for scary medical statistics. The CDC reported

Incorporating bicycling into one's routine is a powerful force in the battle against obesity.

in late 2010 that 26 percent of Americans had a body mass index of more than 30. That's approximately 72 million fat people.

Body mass index is a fancy way of telling you to divide your weight by your height. Putting the high body fat index crisis another way, of every four people you see, at least one of them will be carrying the equivalent of an extra lead-filled volleyball around his hips or waist. (For the record, our body mass indexes are in the low 20s, which is proof you should be biking.)

Now we get to the part that is meant to scare you about obesity. We'll further our lead volleyball image. If you have a lead volleyball handy, strap it to your side or bellybutton and try walking up a flight of stairs. We'll wait for you at the top. ...

We're waiting, waiting.

Should we call 911?

It is no secret that obese people subject their hearts to a lot more stress than people who are not overweight. That lead volleyball on your hips or waist is difficult to carry. Your heart has to pump harder to get you moving. To be sure, a sedentary lifestyle—much desk sitting, little exercise—is only part of the problem. If you're fat, it usually means that you also haven't been eating right. You've been ingesting too many saturated fats, an essential component of potato chips, ice cream, and other staples of the great American diet.

Saturated fat clogs the arteries and vessels that keep blood circulating. Think of it as sludge. The less you exercise, the thicker the sludge, and the more difficult it becomes to exercise, and you exercise even less. Meanwhile, you're inactive body is adding fat. If the sludge stops moving or is reduced to a trickle, an occurrence signaled often by discomfort in your chest and arm, you are having a heart attack.

At worst, a heart attack will kill you, which is obviously bad. Or it will leave you with a compromised circulatory system and necessitate angioplasties, bypass surgeries, and other procedures. An analysis of 57 studies by the Institute for Health Metrics and Evaluation at the University of Washington found that if you're a little fat, you'll live two to five years less, and if you're very fat, you'll live eight to 10 years less.

This will definitely cut into your cycling time.

Fat offers other gifts while you're living, too. It can make you more susceptible to hypertension and high blood pressure, which may lead to stroke and heart disease. It has been linked to an increased likelihood of cancer and even Alzheimer's. Four studies published in the *Journal of the American Medical Association* found strong ties between obesity and declines in mental functioning, including dementia.

Obesity has also been connected to increases in adult onset diabetes, an inability to process blood sugars. Type 2 diabetes, which leads to cardiac disease, cancer, amputation stemming from circulatory problems, and other big medical problems, has been raging nationwide with many urban communities at the forefront. The most recent National Health and Nutrition

Examination survey found that about 2 percent of people with body mass indexes of 25 to 29 had diabetes, while 13 percent of those with a BMI of 35 or more were diabetic. The U.S. Department of Health and Human Services produced the survey.

The fatter you are, the more likely you'll have diabetes.

Obese people who don't exercise suffer from mood swings, insomnia, digestive problems, a higher risk of dying in a car accident because they're closer to the steering wheel, and reduced sexual urges. They will spend about $1,500 per year more on medical fees. Americans spend about $300 billion nationwide on obesity-related care. We could pin the rise of childhood obesity on obese adults, too. Who do you think the kids are learning their exercise and eating habits from?

We summarize: if you are not riding a bike, you will be more likely to become obese, which will cause you to die younger, lose your money, go unintentionally celibate, and set a bad example to children.

Your Trek is waiting.

Can Cycling Really Make You Healthier?

Anything safe that gets you moving is good for your health.

On a bicycle you'll do lots of moving—mostly uninterrupted moving, the best kind.

Los Angeles urban cyclist Jonathan West rides about 35 minutes on each side of his commute from Glendale to Hollywood. That's an hour and 10 minutes of daily exercise. And it is exercise.

West does very little stopping or coasting along the way. He knows which streets have the fewest lights to interrupt his cadence. He climbs a hill or two. He speeds up on boulevards

A bicycle commute can provide 30 minutes or more of uninterrupted movement, an excellent form of exercise. (J. MAUS/BIKEPORTLAND)

that require him to merge with cars. Merging—not riding on sidewalks—is what you're supposed to do when there's not enough room to cycle on the right side. Los Angeles bike messenger and all-around cycling guy Izzy Cortes rides about eight times that distance on busy days, often at rapid speeds.

Pedaling faster increases your heart rate, keeps sludge from accumulating in your circulatory sewer lines, and forces you to use more energy.

Can Cycling Really Help You Lose Weight?

Yes it can, especially if you ride at a good clip without stopping.

The more you move in a particular time, the more energy you'll expend per minute. More energy equals more calories burned.

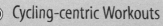

Cycling-centric Workouts

Whether you want to keep your cycling muscles loose in the winter or you just want a new break to your workouts, here are some suggestions for altering your gym workouts to prepare for everyday cycling.

Simply riding a stationary bike may burn some calories, but it hardly goes far in strengthening your muscles to give you a better ride in the long run.

Joy Miles, who has competed for years in marathons and triathlons, is a certified personal trainer and group exercise instructor at Fitness Formula Club in Chicago and urges her students to keep it simple when creating a workout regimen. She tells clients to focus on the major muscle groups used in cycling and to work simple exercises around those muscle groups.

Novice gym members may focus on lifting weights, but Miles cautions against such simple approaches. In fact, Miles urges all cyclists to realize there is more to improving your body than just working your legs. In fact, Miles points out that there are three distinct body groups that your cycling-centric workouts should address: lower body, upper body, and the core.

Lower Body

The major muscle groups of the lower body that are used in cycling are quadriceps, hamstring, calves, hip flexors, gluteus maximus (butt), and soleus (calves). To strengthen each muscle group, Miles suggests that cyclists use a combination of weight-training exercises. **Squats** (quads, hamstrings, soleus, glutes, and hip flexors) involve all the muscles as well as many in your back, but before attempting squats receive proper instruction from a trainer as improper form can lead to problems, particularly in the back. Other lower-body exercises to consider adding to your workout include the following:

leg lifts (abductor/adductor)

lunges (quads, glutes, soleus)

step ups (quads, hamstrings, hip flexors, soleus)

hamstring curls using a stability ball

"In addition, do some balance work on a Bosu Trainer," Miles said, "to help with ankle strength, especially for cyclists who are using clipless pedals."

The number of repetitions per set and the number of sets per workout vary from person to person. But one simple approach is this—for the first week of your workouts just do two sets of each exercise with whatever weight you can do five times to get used to the weight and the exercise movements. After that first week, increase your workout to three sets for each exercise per workout doing whatever weight you can do eight times. From this point, you will do three sets of each exercise per workout, but your reps will increase by one each week until you can do three sets of 15 reps per workout. To go from three sets of 8 to three sets of 15 will take eight weeks if you simply increase your reps by 1 each week.

When you feel comfortable with three sets of 15 and feel you can handle more weight, simply increase your weight by 5 or 10 pounds and start back again doing three sets of 8, working toward three sets of 15 with the weight. Keep repeating this if you wish to increase the weight you're lifting or simply stay at the weight you feel comfortable with if you want.

Upper Body

Anyone who has experienced the jostles and jolts everyday cyclists go through on city streets knows that your upper body can fatigue as quickly as your legs.

That means upper-body workouts are just as important for cyclists as their lower-body and core workouts.

Miles suggests the following upper-body workout exercises:

planks (abdominals, transverse abdominus, erector spinae, and obliques)

push-ups (pectoralis major, triceps, deltoids, latissimus dorsi)

upright rows (deltoid, trapezius, biceps, brachioradialis)

lat pulldowns (lattisimus dorsi, rhomboids)

deadlift (erector spinae, gluteus maximus, adductor magnus, quadriceps, soleus, lower and upper trapezius, levator scapulae, rhomboid, rectus abdominus, and obliques)

We would strongly urge anyone attempting to do deadlifts to get instruction on how to do them properly from a trainer. Generations of athletes have regarded the deadlift as one of the best overall exercises one can use because it works nearly every part of your body. However, when done incorrectly, the deadlift can cause back problems. We know several athletes who refuse to deadlift again because they feel that even though they were given proper instruction, they still experienced back pain. It is a great total-body exercise, just be sure to get instruction first.

The Core

This buzz term has become the rage in the past decade in workout circles, and with good reason. The "core" is basically your torso. The theory goes that if you strengthen your torso, your arms and legs have no alternative but to get in shape, too. In effect, your torso or "core" is the engine of the train, and your arms and legs are train cars being pulled by the force of your engine.

In layman's terms, you are working your abs, back, love handles, shoulders, and lats. Some of the basic core-training exercises include the following:

crunches (rectus abdominus, external and internal obliques)

cable chops (lats, external and internal obliques, traverse abdominus, trunk flexor)

reverse chops (iliocostalis thoracis/loborum, interspinalis, quadratus lomborum, traversus abdominis)

Russian twist (rectus abdominus, transverse abdominus, erector spinae)

"The one thing I would strongly suggest would be to incorporate yoga, Pilates, or some other core-strengthening class to help with cycling," Miles said.

Core training is so vital to overall health that if you pay attention you'll notice that nearly every professional trainer will incorporate core training into workout regimens. They may not use the words *core training,* but when you are working on your torso you are incorporating core training.

A great book to check out is *The Core Performance* by Mark Verstegen. It offers a comprehensive explanation of core training.

Cycling is an activity that doesn't let you rest because if you stop pedaling, you will no longer be upright.

The conclusion: you burn more calories in cycling than other activities because it offers few respites. This is true even if you ride over many hills that allow you to coast downhill. You have to pedal upward to get to the top of the hill, and this part of your ride requires greater exertion than on flat areas. Hence, you burn more calories on the up slope, compensating at least partially for the easier ride down.

We know that there are many diet books that will promise quick routes to a skinnier you. The ones that tell you that you can eat anything amuse us. Based on a quick study of Amazon bestsellers, most diets involve high protein and low carbohydrates, although we know a famous actor who shapes into roles on a strict regimen of lemon juice spiked with cayenne pepper.

Weight loss depends on how many more calories you're burning than consuming. To be more precise, if you expend 3,500 more calories than you ingest, you lose a pound. Star trainer Jillian Michaels could do that for you in a Hollywood minute. But you'd also pay her as much in a month as it would cost to buy a decent bike. Most experts say that you're best off creating a daily 500-calorie deficit—500 more calories burned than consumed—instead of going for the full Monte in a day.

Federal guidelines for healthier living are more relaxed, recommending two hours and 30 minutes of moderate, or one hour and 15 minutes of more vigorous, aerobic activity per week, in a minimum of 10-minutes increments, along with some weight training. Some researchers believe the amount should be more.

A cyclist riding at a reasonable 12-14 mph will burn more than 600 calories per hour, according to our very official accounting—the computer on the Cybex stationary bike at our gym and the several calorie calculators that we found on the Internet. Do that by commuting or running errands or just taking your bike for a quick journey, and then forgo the daily jumbo burger with fries, and you'll start building a calorie deficit.

Okay That Sounds Good, but Don't Other Activities Have More Benefits?

Smart aleck.

One of the few downsides of cycling is that it does not challenge as many muscle groups as other activities. With the exception of a steep uphill when you may briefly stand on your pedals for leverage, you're seated the whole time, and the workout is for your legs. Such sports as basketball, soccer, tennis, and squash have you twisting, swinging, jumping, and moving laterally. Swimming offers an even more concentrated upper-body workout. Even inline skating and running require arm and chest muscles for balancing. With cycling "your resting heart rate is lower," said Pat Etcheberry, an Orlando, Florida–based trainer for some of the world's leading tennis players and golfers.

As an urban cyclist, you'll have difficulty matching the intensities of these other sports because even if you know the signal light calibrations, you will have to slow or stop at some point.

But all this doesn't stamp cycling as second rate. The differences that we cite here are fairly minor. Etcheberry incorporates stationary cycling with other aerobic activities. The former world No. 1 in tennis, Ivan Lendl, famously trained on a high-end road bike between tournaments. (Lendl was not an Etcheberry client.)

As with everything in life, the benefits ultimately depend on how hard you work. If you ride with enough intensity over a long enough distance, you'll improve your cardiovascular fitness and burn calories at a rate comparable with other activities. "All aerobic function can reach the same as far as intensity," said Lauren Harning, a clinical exercise physiologist at the UCLA Medical Center. She added, "You can burn the same

Even professional athletes enjoy bicycling. The bicycle on the right belongs to 7'1" NBA center Joel Przybilla. (J. MAUS/BIKEPORTLAND)

number of calories on a bike as a treadmill. It depends on the exertion and intensity."

Running Doesn't Cost as Much as Cycling. Why Shouldn't I Run?

Do you like your joints?

Knees. Ankles. Lower-back joints.

Running is hard on them. With the knee, when you run, think of two mallets banging against each other with only your little, itsy bitsy cartilage to keep them from hitting each other. Cartilage is remarkable stuff. It can be remarkably resilient. There are 80-year-olds who have almost as much cartilage as some 30-year-olds. But it can also break down quickly via high-impact exercise until the mallets—your bones—are hitting each other. That is called arthritis, and it makes you move like Dick van Dyke dancing with the cartoon penguins in *Mary*

Poppins—lots of mincing, little steps. Van Dyke's excuse is that he had his waistband around his knees, hip-hop style.

Cycling is low impact. Your feet hit the ground only for stopping. You can go for an hour or two and not feel the discomfort that comes with a hard run. "The major benefit of cycling is that it's non–weight bearing," said Lauren Harning. "It's not as much pressure on your knees, hips, ankles, or feet as walking or jogging."

What About Swimming?

Do you have a lake in your backyard?

We knew of a lady who was famous for swimming Los Angeles' Venice Canals, which allegedly were cleaned of all the drug paraphernalia, decaying food, and assorted goodies during the 1990s. We still said, "Yech." We have a rule about touching any body of relatively still water inside city limits.

As for pools, although Southern California and Florida zoning seem to require them of every home, most of us don't have one. The corner hydrant with a New York Fire Department spray nozzle doesn't count. That means you will have to go to a YMCA or other health club, which means that you will need to allocate time for getting there, changing into a swim outfit, and then—because pools are usually much in demand among lap swimmers—have to wait for your turn to do a mile. Then you will have to shower off the chlorine, change, and travel to where you have to go. We find this type of routine bothersome, and if you're traveling by car, we see a huge, unnecessary addition to your carbon footprint.

You could cycle to the pool and burn as many calories.

But That Means That I'll Have to Buy a Bike

And ... ?

That should be the hardest commitment you'll ever have to make. We'll tell you a few things about finding the right bike in another chapter. It doesn't have to set you back a huge amount. Nor will buying a helmet, which we heartily recommend, or the other odds and ends you may decide that you need. In fact, there is such a low threshold to getting started that we'd almost like to make up something so you'll feel as if you've overcome grave obstacles to become a cyclist.

This would enhance your sense of accomplishment.

But the ease with which you can cycle is one of its greatest advantages. Fitness studies through the years have repeatedly shown that people are more apt to start and stay with activities that don't require a lot of effort to pursue. With cycling, you don't have to purchase special clothes or travel to a pool, park, or court.

The workout starts the minute you mount the bike. You pick your route, allocate your time, buckle your helmet, and you're off. We know many people who weren't great athletes or workout warriors, and they've become avid cyclists.

Take the writer and performer Bob Odenkirk, who decided a few years ago that he needed to get in better shape. Odenkirk wasn't a big workout guy. But he had a mountain bike and started using it for five-mile round-trips from his home to the Hollywood Observatory. The 1,000' uphill is the same that Lance Armstrong rode when he stayed in Los Angeles, so it requires some effort.

Now 20 pounds lighter, Odenkirk looks Tour de France ready.

Is That All?

You'll be doing something in the fresh air, which we think is a far better place to ride than in a gym. We would add that limited exposure to the sun's ultraviolet rays helps generate Vitamin D in your skin. Vitamin D has a number of benefits, including the prevention of certain cancers. It can also make you happier, although we know of a number of people who ride happily through the cloud cover and rain bursts of Seattle and the two Portlands—Maine and Oregon. Our grandmothers also always told us that fresh air is good for the complexion.

Cycling is helpful for your social life. Sports create their own communities, and cycling is no different. Cyclists are quick to size up and discuss each other's bikes, share routes, and recommend restaurants and shops along the way. They congregate easily, too—witness the success of bicycle cooperatives in Los Angeles, San Francisco, Salt Lake City, and other cities to help low-income riders. Last fall, we road Los Angeles' first CicLAva event, which continues a tradition started in Bogota,

A cyclist takes in cherry blossom season in Portland. Exposure to fresh air and Vitamin D from the sun are just two of bicycling's health benefits. (J. MAUS/BIKEPORTLAND)

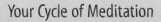

Your Cycle of Meditation

One surprising, positive side effect of cycling daily alongside tons of vehicles while dodging potholes and yawning car doors is a truly relaxed mental state known as "walking meditation." It has been a part of Taoist, Buddhist, and Christian rituals for thousands of years.

Ancient labyrinths built into medieval cloisters created structured environs where Catholic clergy could practice walking meditation by walking the maze while praying the rosary. Eastern religions used this practice centuries earlier, recognizing that some people reacted better to rhythmic exercise, rather than seated meditation, to reach deep meditation. The theory is that repetitive exercise frees the mind from the daily world's static.

"When we do walking meditation, we are using the physical, mental, and emotional experiences of walking as the basis of developing greater awareness," explains wildmind.org, a Buddhist meditation website. "Practicing walking meditation is a way of 'de-fragmenting' our minds. One of the literal meanings of the word *sati* (usually translated as 'mindfulness') is 'recollection.' In practicing mindfulness we are 're-collecting' the fragmented parts of our psyches, and reintegrating them into a whole. As we become more whole, we become more contented and more fulfilled. This is one of the main benefits and aims of the practice of mindfulness."

Of course, we're replacing walking with cycling, but that's the point. Any exercise can work for this type of meditation.

You have probably experienced this type of meditation when exercising and didn't realize it. Being in the zone while working out or feeling a jogger high is part of this phenomenon.

Two things are happening simultaneously. Physically, your body excretes endorphins when you exercise, and their chemical release into your blood system triggers feelings of euphoria and happiness. Mentally, your mind is suddenly freed from the shackles of serious thought everyday life requires (job, family, bills, etc.) and able to appreciate everything it is experiencing.

So the next time you're cycling and the rhythm of your pumping legs falls into sync with your breathing and you no longer are thinking about your life but rather simply enjoying it, you are experiencing a glimpse into walking meditation.

Columbia, of mass, one-day street closings for cyclists. More than 10,000 other cyclists pedaled along streets usually heavy with traffic in Hollywood and downtown. Participants smiled. Police smiled. And every few blocks we noticed cyclists prone in front of restaurants, downing takeout dishes from local eateries and enjoying a shared interest. Happier people are healthier.

It Seems Like a lot of Effort

No it isn't.

And that's the great part. You don't have to do anything special. You get exercise without trying to get exercise—on the way to the store, the bank, to school, to work. Boston cyclist Mark Halliday has controlled his weight for years as a result of his 20-mile round-trip commutes. Chris Rommelmann has kept in shape for his acting and stunt work largely by getting around on a bike. Rommelmann is one of those rarities: a bicoastal urban cyclist. He works in Los Angeles and New York, so he keeps bikes in both cities.

A Final Question

What sort of person are you?

Are you the follower of trends or an individualist? If you cycle, you're the latter. For all the reasons we outline in these pages—environment, health, economics, good times—you've chosen a particular lifestyle. In itself this is a health benefit. We believe that people are happiest when they chase experiences of their own choosing rather than waiting passively for things to happen. They are doing their planning, setting the terms of their engagement, and supplying the creativity. The sense of satisfaction is fuller.

3

Bike Buying

How to Survive by Buying the Right Bike

Bike buying is where you get to have some fun before you get to have fun.

That's because you get to spend money.

We hope that you can spend lots of it, or at least afford exactly the bicycle you want.

But you will be more inclined to ride a bicycle that you feel good on. We mean that from a psychic as well as a physical standpoint. The latter is clearly more important—we'll get to fit and feel shortly.

At the same time, psychic benefits are not to be underestimated.

We now hearken you to your elementary and junior high school years when you probably purchased your first grown-up bicycle. That means the wheels were about 26". The graduation to a 26" wheel is the bicycle version of a Bar or Bat Mitzvah. Our Bike Mitzvah came via the European or Japanese 10-speed, steel bikes that were hot items in the '70s and '80s. We received a French Peugot just before we started seventh grade. Needless to say, we were eager to show it off at school.

Here's our point. We were kids, but showing off is part of everyone's DNA, adults included. It applies equally for a $1,650 Trek Portland, a pricy urban cycle, as it does for a $60,000 Mercedes E-class sedan. We've been showing off our multi-colored, very comfortable Happy Socks of late. Satisfaction does not depend on value.

A beloved purchase makes you feel strong, sophisticated, tasteful, cool, hip, or some quality that you want desperately to be a big part of your identity. For some members of the serious bicycling community, purchasing the latest gear satisfies a desire to float ahead of the gear curve.

Of course, I need the $7,000 Cervelo R5 with Squoval, Smartwall, and an optimized head tube taper.

And that language is?

These are the names for features that enable the high-end manufacturer Cervelo to produce light, aerodynamic frames that 99-something percent of riders will never need. People who train long distances on bikes devour them.

Racer. Trickster. Casual rider. Commuter.

You buy what you are.

There's nothing wrong with that. You don't have to mount a certain bike because someone else says it's better than the one you've been eyeing. Who knows better than you what you need?

When you feel good about your acquisition, you'll be happier and prouder on your bike.

We consider that a psychic boon.

It will make you more likely to use your bike.

We consider increased bike usage a tangible benefit resulting from the psychic benefit of feeling good.

The right bike selection is a big part of becoming an urban cyclist.

We'll tell you a little bit about bike shopping with the caveat that this is not a comprehensive guide or in-depth analysis of models. *Bicycling* magazine and a bike-load of websites have bike reviewing down to a science.

Selection

You'll have a lot of choices. How many? So many that the best folks in this country for analyzing the bike industry have never calculated how many models there are. What they can say is that bike companies sold approximately 20 million bikes in 2010 and that there were 149 brands. "The number of brands hasn't changed appreciably in the last six years," said Jay Townley, a founding partner of the Gluskin-Townley Group, a marketing and research consultancy that tracks the U.S. bicycle industry.

Each company has multiple models. Multiple, multiple models. Take Trek, which sells more bicycles at U.S. bike retail stores than any other brand. On its website, Trek has 11 categories of bikes. That's categories!

In its road division, it has 11 subcategories or series. Not bikes but categories of road bikes that address different audiences. The FX series, a potential option for urban cyclists, goes 15 models strong. Prices range from $450 to almost $3,000. Its hard-tail, or front shock absorber, mountain bike division has another 11 series, including a bicycle used by the New York Police Department. Trek has 11 series in its urban division and another half dozen in what it calls its bike path division. The latter includes 12 city-ready hybrid models. We're missing a few divisions here, but take our word: the Waterloo, Wisconsin–based company has listings covering more than 100 bicycles that would do fine on city streets.

We estimated about 50 bike models on the website of Specialized, another big brand in U.S. cycling. Even a niche brand like Electra offers six series of bikes. Located just north of San Diego in a quiet industrial park, the company manufactures upright, European-style bicycles, beach cruisers, and tandem bicycles. Electra has risen up the ranks in sales and popularity in recent years, partly because of renewed interest in city cycling. "They have positioned themselves nicely among the top 10 brands," said Townley.

Let's say very conservatively that the country's 149 bike brands sell an average of six models. Then we'd have approximately 900 models from which you can choose. And that doesn't include department store bikes sold at the marts, K- and Wal-, Toys-R-Us, Target, or Costco. Department stores sold about seven in every eight bicycles in 2010—roughly 17.5 million bikes.

It doesn't include the tiny but steady segment of custom bikes. Remember the $7,000 Cervelo we mentioned. We're not sure how someone could improve on it for lightness and speed. A top-grade Cervelo weighs about as much as the computer we're writing on. But we figure that if you can throw enough money at a supreme bike craftsman, you can get something even more special.

High-end custom or noncustom bikes are obviously overkill for most people just looking for a comfortable ride. Then again, if you've just won the lottery, we'd love to see you go crazy on a bicycle rather than buy the Mercedes.

Serviceable Options

As an urban cyclist, you'll probably be choosing from five types of bicycles. They are touring, mountain, hybrid, fold-up, or city bicycles. That is not to discourage the nonconformist. If you want to ride to work on a beach cruiser, recumbent cycle, titanium racer, home-brewed fixie, or adult tricycle, count us among the first to cheer you on. Jay Townley rode a mountain bike when he was a Schwinn executive years ago, the better to navigate Chicago's deep potholes and steep curbs. (He rides a no-longer manufactured Ryan recumbent now in the Wisconsin countryside.) Safety Cycle head mechanic Diego Souza rides a fixie. Los Angeles bicycling advocate and former shop owner Steve Hoffman prefers a gray, six-speed fold-up Yeah that he rescued from the street and rehabbed. Yeah focuses entirely on fold-up bikes. Hoffman's other bikes include vintage, 4-speed Schwinn Crate and Racer bikes, the latter a 1961 model. We could find people nationally cycling on almost everything imaginable.

In short, we believe anything that gets you riding regularly is good.

Cycling is the sport of mavericks, oddballs, eccentrics, outcasts, rebels, loners, free spirits, and mountain men coming in for supplies.

And we mean all those descriptors in a good way.

But the five bike types are generally best suited for daily or near-daily city cycling. They are usually rugged enough and have wider—sometimes much wider—tires to absorb bumps. For the most part, they allow for easier attachment of panniers, baskets, and racks. They allow the rider to sit in the sort of upright position that most average riders favor for reasons of comfort. Because they are sold more widely than other models, there is a huge range of prices. You can find a serviceable hybrid new for under $300.

What's serviceable?

For us that means simply the bicycle, without any special attention on a daily basis, will get you where you want to go efficiently and safely just about every time you hop on. We make allowances for the occasional carpet tack–induced tire puncture and equipment malfunction that can happen with any bicycle. That doesn't mean that the ride will be Cadillac quality, that the bicycle will wow people with its aesthetic, or that the parts will last as long as with more expensive models. Quality parts and materials are where you lose with inexpensive bicycles. They don't fit together as tightly, and they wear faster, sometimes much faster. "Generally, the patents for less expensive bike equipment are identical to the most expensive equipment," said Larry Hoffman. "They are the same except the connectors and materials aren't as good. Wearing time won't be as long. The cheaper they are, the less they'll last."

Hoffman owned the North Hollywood Pedal Shop for the better part of three decades, assembled a book on safe riding for the Los Angeles Police Department, and helped expand the city's network of cycling lanes. By his estimate, he has sold and repaired tens of thousands of bikes—and still does the latter with a multi-tool he keeps handy. He also continues to track cycling trends. In his opinion, the good news is that the quality of bicycles has improved significantly since he first started his business. He says that it is now easy to find a solidly built bicycle at much lower prices than ever. That's largely because of advances in manufacturing technology and materials. "Almost all bikes are serviceable," Hoffman said. "They'll get you where you want to get."

Consider your fears of purchasing a lemon allayed, although Hoffman says that while you can find a serviceable bicycle at a department store, you should take it to a specialty store after purchase. Department or big-box store bikes do not often receive the loving attention as those at bikes-only shops, and so may not be assembled carefully. "Sometimes deals are out there, but if you purchase from a department store at least bring the bike to a reputable bike store to make sure everything is all right and tuned up. I've always told people, 'spend the extra money for the quick tune-up.'"

The five different types of bicycles we mentioned earlier all have advantages and disadvantages. Depending on the material, technology, and other variables, even bicycles within the same category will ride differently and have pluses and minuses. We will say more on this latter topic shortly. What's important for now is not to fret about these differences, or believe that one type of bicycle is inherently better riding, cooler, or superior to others.

If you pull a single wisdom from this chapter, it is that there is no best bike. The $800, eight-gear city bicycle may feel better and be easier to ride than a $1,500, 24-gear mountain bike. The $5,000 carbon extravaganza hanging like a prized turkey in a shop window will probably feel worst of all. Top racing bikes are known for speed not comfort. We'll tackle the general goods and bads for each category as we go.

The best bike for you is the one that meets your needs and budget.

Most importantly, it's the one that fits and feels best.

Touring

Touring bikes look a lot like their racing cousins. So much, that if you were to replace the more mundane-sounding brand names on their bottom tubes with exotic Italian ones, at quick glance, you'd be hard-pressed to distinguish them from something you'd see at the Tour de California. Most major multiproduct manufacturers offer several models. They generally include 20-plus gears, caliper brakes, and steel or aluminum frames. Some may include carbon forks. You'll have a choice between drop-down (ram's horn) or straight handlebars. You can add extension bars—perpendicular, pen-length add-ons—that will allow you to vary your riding position. Extension bars will help ward off the stiffness coming from sitting in the exact same position for hours.

Advantages: These are bicycles that are made for people who bicycle long distances. They are sturdier and have wider tires than racing bikes, but some of the better touring bicycles aren't much heavier. One touring bike participant in a BikeForum.net string some years ago described catching a younger cyclist despite riding with grocery-filled panniers. Another writer described his touring bike as "A Jack of All Trades." "You can carry TONS of weight on them, ride long distances with reasonable comfort, commute within 1-2 mph of my road bike speed ..." Touring bikes easily accommodate panniers and baskets. They are much lighter than hybrids, city bikes, and mountain bikes—and faster.

Disadvantages: A good touring bike may be much more than you need, particularly if you won't be traveling long distances. Touring bikes cost as much as some racers and on average are more expensive than mountain bikes and hybrids. A touring bike with a drop bar may not be the most comfortable option.

Mountain Bikes

These are stocky, durable bicycles with straight handlebars and lots of gears—usually 24-plus. Mountain bikes were the brainchild of a group of San Francisco area riders who wanted something heavier duty for tackling the surrounding area's dirt trails. Their popularity exploded in the late 1980s and '90s amidst soaring

Mountain bike with thick tires and front shocks.

interest in outdoor sports, although with time many purchasers were city dwellers who liked their rugged look. Mountain bikes are best known for their thick, aluminum top tubes and wide, nobby tires, the better for gripping uneven surfaces. This feature has proven as good at absorbing the imperfections of city streets as wilderness paths. Mountain bikes fall into three categories. Rigids do not have shock absorbers and resemble hybrids. Hard-tails have front shocks. Dual-shock bikes have shock absorbers over the front and back wheels. They were designed to absorb the punishment of steep, bumpy downhill courses. Shocks of any sort are probably not needed for urban riding.

Advantages: Provided you care for it well, the average mountain bike bought at a retail store will last about as long as the ice age. The thick tires will cushion you on rough roads. The aluminum frame won't rust in wet weather and will with-stand heavy weight.

Disadvantages: These bikes are generally heavier than touring bikes and more plodding. This is partly due to the frame weight but also because knobby tires don't have as much surface contacting the road as smoother tires. That said, some urban cyclists exchange knobby for smoother tires. Aluminum frames tend to be stiffer and less comfortable than steel frames. Dual-shock bikes are among the heaviest bikes on the market.

Hybrids

Hybrids are a cross between touring and mountain bikes. They are solid, durable bikes, well suited for urban riding. Hybrid top tubes and frames are thicker than those on touring bikes but less so than those on mountain bikes. In the width and tread smoothness, hybrid tires fall between touring and mountain bike tires. Hybrids have straight handlebars and riders sit in an upright position, roughly the same as they would on a mountain bike. Most hybrids won't have shocks.

Advantages: For the money, these bikes offer good value. They'll withstand the rigors of city travel and offer a reasonably comfortable ride. They are also easy to load with carrying devices.

Disadvantages: If you're looking for fancy, go elsewhere. You can also find faster and more comfortable bicycles, particularly the latter, if you opt for some city and mountain bikes.

City Cycles

These bicycles are patterned after European upright bikes. Many of them have internal hubs, the better to protect gearing mechanisms from inclement weather. More expensive city bikes have seven or eight gears. City bikes' simple, solid constructions also look at home with panniers and baskets, bells, and tire guards. Most city bikes are made of steel.

Advantages: You'll earn points for cool. The heavy frames are durable and practical for commutes and short trips. We are fans of Electra's Amsterdam and Townie models. They are heavy but elegant, appointed in tasteful colors with just enough

City upright-style bike with internal hub.

gearing to climb normal inclines. Electra was the brainchild of a couple of recent European immigrants who were looking for bikes similar to those with which they grew up. The company's retro vibe caught Hollywood's attention in the early 2000s, and a former Schwinn executive is now overseeing the firm's growth. Specialized's Globe division, Linus, Abici, Work Cycles, and Batavus are among other manufacturers of city bicycles.

Women's city bike with fenders and rear rack.

Disadvantages: You won't be able to go fast. Steep hills may be a problem for people who aren't fit. If you don't use your bicycle much, you risk being called an urban cycling imposter or worse, a hipster. Our remedy is to add a cosmetic mark or two. Better yet, use the bike.

Fixed-Gear and Other Bikes

With fixed-gear bicycles, the sprocket—toothy disk—connects directly to the rear-wheel hub. All you have to know is that the bike moves only when you pedal. There is no free rear wheel. If you pedal backward, you don't coast but instead go backward. In recent years, fixies have become more popular in cities. Their boosters, generally young men, say fixies offer a purer riding experience because the bicycle responds directly to everything they do. There are no gears to make hill climbing easier. The bike has been stripped to bare essentials. Add about 30 pounds to the modern fixie frame, and you're riding the same system as nineteenth-century safety cyclists. Do not confuse the true fixie with freewheel, single-speed bicycles. Freewheel bikes won't have multiple gears, but you'll be able to pedal backward and coast.

Coaster bikes offer another single-speed option. This is the sort of bike that we knew first. You stop by reverse pedaling. Stop hard and you leave cool skid marks. Many beach cruisers are also coasters. These are bikes with curved top tubes and handlebars that hook slightly back. Most people associate cruisers with surfboard-carrying Southern Californians on boardwalks. But they can also serve as effective urban bicycles for people who travel short distances.

Advantages: Single speeds are often lightweight and easy to maneuver. They stamp you as a serious cyclist, or as someone who is sensible enough to know that cyclists don't need much

Fixed-gear bicycle with upturned handlebars.

to ride. Fixed speeds can be assembled inexpensively in repair co-ops that carry donated frames. A scruffed up fixie may not garner as much attention from thieves. If you're going through a midlife crisis, or want to become political about bicycles, they'd be appropriate for group rides with Critical Mass. The sometimes rabble-rousing movement organizes monthly rides to promote cyclists' rights, and other causes.

Disadvantages: We'll say the obvious: if you live or work on a precipitous slope, or haven't been working out much, fixed or single-gear bicycles won't be your best option. Then again, a fixie might be just what you need to get in shape. Fixies aren't usually aesthetically remarkable. Pedaling and braking may feel awkward.

Fold-Ups

These are bikes to fold up into one or more sections via a hinge or hinges on the frame. They are built for adults, but the wheels are almost cartoonishly small. Dahon is the recognizable brand in the fold-up market. The company was the brainchild of a

Fold-up bike.

Hughes Aircraft Corporation physicist, David Hon, whose research on laser technology has been used in weaponry. In the 1970s, Hon quit his job to work on projects that would better society. Struck by the world's dependence on oil, he began applying his energies to the creation of a more portable bicycle. Hon believed such a bike would allow a wider group of people—those who could consistently cycle-commute directly from their homes and those mixing public transportation with cycling—to cycle as a more frequent means of transportation. Bike companies rejected building or licensing his prototype, so he set up his own company in the early 1980s. Dahon now offers more than 50 models. The company sells approximately 100,000 bicycles a year, said Jay Townley, and has continued to introduce innovations. Recent Dahon frames have included holders for iPads and mobile phone gear. "It is the premier brand in the fold-up market because it's been around the longest," Townley said, adding, "David and his company are part of the urban bicycle movement."

Most Dahons come with 20-inch wheels. Most adult bicycles have wheels that measure 26 inches or a little larger than that. Dahon also produces bikes with 16-, 24-, and 26-inch wheels. Yeah Bicycles' wheels range from a tiny 14 to 26 inches. Shimano, Schwinn, and Brompton manufacture fold-up bikes, too. We hesitate to mention, but in recent years, a few companies have begun offering electric fold-ups. They operate via rechargeable batteries. Our analysis of electric bikes is if you're going to cycle, then cycle.

Advantages: Fold-ups are easier to store than traditional bikes. That's an advantage if you don't have a lot of storage space. It's also a plus if you want flexibility in commuting. If the weather worsens and you decide that you don't want to cycle home, it's easier to carry your bike on public transportation or throw it in the trunk of a taxi. The same portability will allow you to take your bike on vacations. Some people have doubts about the durability of fold-ups, but we've seen one used by a veteran cyclist on long tours. He loads his bicycle with panniers and even connects a trailer to it. When he wants to take the train, he slips the fold-up into the trailer. By the way, it can take anywhere from a few seconds to several minutes to fold up a fold-up. By Dahon estimates, the company's road fold-up, a Flo X20, will take 15 minutes to fold.

Disadvantages: You won't be able to go fast as easily. There are more parts on the frame, which increases the potential for something going awry. Some models can be difficult to fold.

Steel versus Aluminum (versus Composite)

When you get set to buy a bicycle, you will most likely face one decision regarding frame materials: steel versus aluminum. You will only consider carbon or titanium if you want to pay for the sensation of riding a super-light bike whose advantages are disproportionate to your needs as an urban cyclist. We know of only one cyclist, former Olympian Ron Skarin, who rode a composite fiber bike to work, and that was more because top-flight bikes were part of his life. He advised one company on construction of a titanium model in the 1980s. Forget adding panniers or baskets to a composite bike. Would you tie a trailer to a Porsche?

We're not going to delve into detail here about how steel and aluminum compare. The admirable SheldonBrown.com offers a reader-friendly analysis of these materials' stiffness, strength, and weight. Brown points out that any comparison is meaningless if you're assuming the diameter of frame parts—the tubing—is the same because you would not use the same diameter tubing for a steel frame as you would for an aluminum one.

Generally speaking, fatter-tubed aluminum frames of the type you'll find on many mountain bikes feel stiffer. By stiffer we mean the frame doesn't seem to absorb roads' bumpiness as well as a more flexible frames. But not every aluminum frame feels stiffer than every steel frame. And a stiff frame doesn't always mean less comfort. Some people may prefer stiffer frames. Aluminum is also a lighter material by nature, although advances in technology have allowed manufacturers to build comparably light steel frames.

We ride thick-tubed mountain bikes ourselves, but we're far from advocating for aluminum. We are great admirers of steel frames, including frames marketed as chromoly, short for chromium molybdenum. Chromoly is a high-grade steel alloy that is commonly found on city bikes. Chromoly bikes look good and can last a long time. We know many people who are happy with their steel bikes.

Steel bikes rust, which may be a disadvantage if you're living in areas of heavy rainfall. But then again, if you care about your bike, you're not going to leave it in damp conditions for prolonged periods. After parking your bike in the rain, wipe it down as soon as you're somewhere dry.

Our words of wisdom on choice of materials:

Test a number of bikes. Choose the one that feels best, not the one that you think you're supposed to buy.

It's your bike.

Your decision.

Big Box versus Specialist

We shop regularly at Target. We've found great bargains there. The bikes sold in Target and other department stores are inexpensive. They're safe and reliable for getting you where you need to without incident, if not comfortably. Department store bikes have improved to the point where some are probably the equal of less costly products sold in bike specialty shops.

However, we wouldn't buy a bike at any department store unless we needed a quick fix—not fixie—or children's bike that was soon to be outgrown.

This is why.

Department stores are always looking for deals that they can pass on to customers, which makes the customers happy that they are spending less money and keeps them coming back. This is capitalism. The stores are able to do this by purchasing large volumes of product. But the products are usually of lesser quality. Here's where we get to pick on the rising economic juggernaut of China. We have nothing against Chinese industriousness. Some Americans could learn a thing or two about the Chinese work ethic. The Chinese build a lot of cheap bikes—often under other people's names—and send them to the U.S. The downside of all this is that the parts are inferior to those on higher-level bicycles. They may wear down quickly, requiring you to replace them or seek a new bike. Slowly, the money you've saved evaporates.

Here's another reason we wouldn't buy our bicycle at a department store. The bikes arrive in big boxes. They are usually only partly assembled or require some tightening and tinkering to get them into shape. The department store assigns someone to this task—if they assign anyone at all. In some cases, this individual simply places the bike on display. In other instances, this person attaches the missing pieces and exhibits the finished product. He may be perfectly nice and smart. But he is probably not a bike person. He has probably come over from household appliances or the electronics section. Los Angeles bicycle advocate Steve Hoffman recommends taking department store bikes to a bike shop for a tune-up, even if you've just purchased it. We think you'd be better starting at the bike shop, even if it costs a little more in the short run.

By the way, that person who assembled the bike usually isn't going to be able to fit you on a frame or suggest different models. You'll be on your own.

Pay for expertise.

In the Shop

Now that we've browbeat you into buying from a bike shop, we'll be the first to tell you that not all shops are created equal. Some cater to one segment of the cycling population or one brand. If you see lots of carbon fiber and Cervelo bicycles, you're probably in a racing shop. If you see lots of Specialized bikes or Globes, their city bike brand, you know that you're at a certified Specialized dealer. This isn't necessarily a bad thing.

Specialized produces lots of fine bikes in every major category. You should be able to find a bike at a Specialized dealer. It will just say Specialized on the frame.

Some shops offer better customer service. Some shops have wider selections. It's the same with any retail operation. It's up to you as the customer to find the shop that serves you best. In our opinion, some things are nonnegotiable. The good news is that the U.S. has roughly 4,178 shops, and we can say, based on a fair sampling of them, that most of them know their business. Still, we thought it would be helpful to compile a list of what you do and don't want in a shop.

First the noes: Shops should not do the following:

- Be impatient no matter how many questions you ask, as self-explanatory as they may seem. *Is a straight handlebar inferior to a drop one? Good question, let me tell you about the merits of each.*

- Push you into a product or rush your decision. A little sound guidance about brands and models is helpful. Too much pressure to purchase a particular bike, or to buy fast, can sour your buying experience. A bike shop's success rests on its reputation. If you're unhappy, you're unlikely to recommend the shop to others.

- Encourage you to buy accessories that you don't need. See the above point on our distaste for the hard sell.

- Blind you with lingo. To paraphrase Shakespeare badly, names are just names. If someone uses them too freely, stop her and ask for an explanation. If she persists, find someone else who can make things understandable. Then renew your focus on whether your bike is going to fit and feel right.

- Keep you waiting to help customers likely to buy more expensive bikes. Customers are customers to be treated equally. Besides, the client who spends less initially may be the one who returns repeatedly, blogs about a good experience, or tells friends. Have patience at busy times— a full shop is a good sign that it does a good job serving its customers. Leave if you feel you're being bypassed or ignored because you don't rank high enough in pecking order.

Yeses: Shops should do the following:

- Treat you with respect and dignity.

- Answer your questions with patience.

- Offer free, new-purchase tune-ups for several weeks, and probably for months. New bicycles often suffer cable stretch and other minor problems. Most bike shops offer return tune-ups as policy.

- Inquire about what type of riding you'll be doing, and along what routes, and then point you to appropriate bikes.

- Keep your budget in mind.

- Fit you properly.

- Allow you to try several bikes.

- Ensure you have the right accessories.

- Smile a lot. Enthusiasm is the best contagion.

Bike Fitting

You wouldn't buy a pair of pants that don't fit you. Why do it for a bike? It's significantly more expensive. And the potential repercussions of an ill-fitting bike are more serious than bad pants. If you're too small or big for your bike, you risk injury. Say the same for your pants, and at worst you look like a rap musician or Michael Jackson in his high-water days.

Too small a frame will not allow you to extend your leg on the down pedal. The continuous cramped motioning may cause knee trouble. Too large a frame will prevent you from striking the pedals with the full force of the right part of your foot and also make you more susceptible to leg injuries. If the distance between the handlebars and seat is off, you may be more vulnerable to back problems. Experienced shop clerks, riders themselves who have done hundreds of fittings, will normally be able to size you up in a few minutes. Then as you try different bikes, they fine-tune their estimates. But many shops use fitting tools to generate precise measurements.

But these measurement systems will not guarantee you mount the perfect bike immediately. You're still going to have to ride a number of bikes to determine which is best. You may still need a saddle adjustment.

We decided to put bike fitting to the test. We wanted to see if one system was superior to another or led to better bike recommendations. We asked three shops to measure us and then suggest some bicycles. Orange20 Cycles, a Los Angeles shop, and the REI in Arcadia, California, used a FitKit system, a series of devices for measuring such key areas as inseam and arm length. Safety Cycle lead salesman Farsh Farrokhnia based his fitting on experience. He's worked in shops for the better part of the last five years and hopes to start his own store one day. At Metropolis Cycles in Los Angeles, we didn't even bother with a formal measurement. We simply asked to test-ride a few of the store's city bikes.

Our first fitting began with Orange 20's Ace Carretero telling us to relax. Carretero, who's been fitting customers with FitKit for more than a year, said if customers are tense, it can skew the analysis. "Getting the person to breathe is important for the true fitting," said Carretero, who has been working in shops for more than five years. That sounded easy enough.

Carretero threw us off when he said that "there's a lot of cushioning" with the FitKit. "It gives you ranges," he said. Wasn't the point that the FitKit would eliminate approximations? Carretero said that the FitKit gave him numerical reinforcement for what he was seeing.

For the FitKit, we stood on a nice piece of polished wood that looked like a shoe measure. The board had two holes at one end, and Carretero inserted a roughly 18" aluminum tube that connected vertically to another piece of wood. The device resembled a surgical cane. Carretero unfastened a lock, and the wooden top rose steadily until it was pressing firmly but not painfully into the bottom part of our crotch. We were 55½ centimeters, which he dutifully wrote on a piece of paper. He took measurements using a smaller but similarly shaped device for our torso, arm length, and foot. The procedure took less than five minutes, allowing for him to record our measurements and compare them to a chart that FitKit provides.

Then Carretero asked us how we use our bike and what we were willing to pay. We told him that we were looking for a bike that we could use for casual street riding or workouts. We wanted something sturdy but also with a little speed. We didn't have a preference of steel or aluminum. Carretero suggested a Janus Quest, a steel frame with a carbon fork—the carbon fork is not unusual on pricier touring and city bikes—and Shimano components. The bike fit perfectly and we liked the style. At $1,700, it was a little pricey. So Carretero recommended a Janus Coda, a flat-bar road bike for $600. It was also a good fit. "The main objective is leading the customer correctly," Carretero said. "You have to get the fit right and read the customer to put him or her on the right bike."

At REI we had the bike department supervisor, Michael Fitzpatrick, fit an 11-year-old relative. The measuring, with a few giggles at the inseam recording, lasted about the same as at Orange 20. Fitzpatrick had a little difficulty finding a bike with the right cockpit combination—saddle to handlebar measurement—for a child. He eventually settled on a Marin Bridgeway or Novaro Forza. Both bikes were a smidgen long, but that was fine with us, given the way 11-year-olds grow.

At Safety Cycle, there were no measuring devices. Farsh Farrokhnia looked us over and then asked a few questions about our riding habits. Farrokhnia recommended a Specialized Allez Double Steel. We test-drove the bike up and down a long alley. Farrohkhnia said that he's able to get a good sense of what will fit just by looking at someone's height and build. We had no complaints.

We didn't have any complaints about the fit of the bikes we tried at Metropolis. Full disclosure: we tried the three-speed, internally hubbed Felt MP in army green, just to see what it felt like to ride what the salesman described as the "Hummer of bikes." Cost: $600. It felt big and bulky—we estimated that it weighed more than 30 pounds—and we experienced a strange guilt, although the Hummer of bikes wasn't fuel burning. The Felt MP wasn't our thing, although the fit was fine. We weren't crazy about the styling of the Schwinn Voyager 21, an aluminum hybrid with front shocks that cost $400. More to our liking were the $700 fixed-gear by Pake with a black and white skull design, and the $750 aluminum Electra Amsterdam Sport.

Conclusions: The three stores did a good job of fitting us and finding bikes that would meet our specifications—style- and budget-wise. The FitKit gave us confidence that the sizing would be right, although we are convinced that a good eye will generate satisfactory results. Given our experience at Metropolis, we also believe more than ever that in finding the right bike, the onus rests on the consumer to test-drive models until the right one appears.

4

Helmets

Fifteen Questions About Wearing a Helmet

1. Why Wear a Helmet?

Draw your conclusions from the following reports.

The Insurance Institute for Highway Safety (IIHS) said that 91 percent of cyclists killed in 2008 were reportedly not wearing helmets. A New York City survey of bicycle fatalities from 1996 to 2005 found that three in four cycling fatalities involved a head injury and that 97 percent of cyclists killed were not wearing a helmet.

Neither report came from a helmet advocacy group. The IIHS is a Virginia-based nonprofit scientific and educational organization. The New York City study combined the efforts of the New York Departments of Health and Mental Hygiene, Parks and Recreation, Transportation, and the police department.

One study found that helmets reduce the risk of head injury by 85 percent and brain injury by 88 percent. (J. MAUS/BIKEPORTLAND)

A well documented *New England Journal of Medicine* study found that helmets reduced the risk of head injury by 85 percent and brain injury by 88 percent. The study looked at 235 individuals who had received emergency care for head injuries at local hospitals. The study concluded that "helmets are highly effective in preventing head injury."

Eric Richter, a senior brand manager for Giro, said that helmets are "like airbags…lessening the severity of any injuries that might stem from a head strike or a crash." By wearing a helmet, you reduce the risk of suffering a life-altering injury.

2. Will Helmets Guarantee Your Safety?
Let's dispel any misconceptions.

They will not ensure your survival.

They will not prevent your involuntary transformation into a walking cucumber.

They cannot guarantee that you will escape an accident without a fracture, concussion, contusion, scrapes, scratches, bruises, or bad boo-boos on your noggin.

Sometimes It's Better to Be a Woman

If you died in a bicycle accident in 2008, chances are you were a 41-year-old male who was riding in the late afternoon or early evening in the fall and the last thing you did before leaving this mortal coil was approaching or riding through a city intersection.

At least that's the most likely outcome based on the statistical analysis done by the Insurance Institute for Highway Safety and the folks at bicyclinginfo.org.

According to bicyclinginfo.org, the average age for a bicyclist who died in an accident in 2008 was 41, compared to 24 in 1998. In 2008, men represented 87 percent of all bicycling fatalities.

The IIHS supports those findings, citing that every year since 1975 male fatalities have accounted for at least 80 percent of all bicycle fatalities—except for 1977 when the 730 male deaths that year were 79 percent of all cycling fatalities.

September was 2008's worst month for fatalities, according to the IIHS, accounting for 12 percent of all deaths. It was followed by October and August (11 each), May and July (10), and April and June (nine).

Urban locations accounted for 68 percent of 2008 deaths while the remaining 32 percent were in rural locations. Dovetailing with those numbers, 38 percent of all fatalities that year occurred at an intersection.

Finally, the IIHS listed 21 percent of all deaths occurred between 6 PM and 9 PM, followed by the 17 percent who died from 3 PM and 6 PM.

To be clear, helmets are not a panacea. If you hit something hard enough, fall the wrong way, or fail to size a helmet properly, even the best, most scientifically advanced, expensive Bell, Bianchi, Briko, Cratoni, Fuji, Giro, Michelin, Schwinn, or Specialized (to name just a few) won't keep you unscathed. "There are a couple of misperceptions about helmets: One is that a helmet exists to prevent you from splitting open your head or a skull fracture," said Richter of Giro, a division of Easton Bell. The Pennsylvania company is the leading manufacturer of helmets in the U.S. "They will not guarantee prevention of any injury."

3. How Do Helmets Work?

It's not the hardened plastic that protects you as much as the stuff inside. Most of that stuff is made of expanded polystyrene, the same petroleum-based compound used for packing beads. Look at the texture of EPS, as it is often called, in beads and helmets. It looks like tiny balls combined. These balls are molded into larger shapes via heat and pressure. The end product may be the most efficient per gram of any substance in absorbing the force of a blow. When a cyclist is struck in the head, the EPS "crushes," said Giro's Richter. "In crushing, the EPS balls absorb the energy of the impact, rather than having that energy transmitted through your skull and brain. This is why crashed helmets, in addition to compressing, have cracks and other signs of stress and energy dissipation."

Replace Helmet, Not Your Head

One small but important fact that most cyclists do not realize is that if they are unfortunate enough to have an accident that caused them to hit their helmet on anything, they then need to replace it.

We know cyclists who are very stubborn about this topic. It's hard enough to get some cyclists to even wear a helmet, much less replace one. It doesn't matter if you were in a one-bike accident (pothole) or a major collision with a car, if your helmet hit any solid object it has fulfilled it's purpose and must be replaced.

Why?

Helmets are not designed to last forever. They are designed to absorb the impact of a collision so that your skull and the soft tissue of your head do not. The foam of the helmet absorbs the impact. The outer shell of the helmet is a slick plastic so that your head slides along the surface and doesn't get caught, wrenching your neck and making your injuries worse.

4. What's the Right Fit?

Helmet sizing isn't like measuring for a suit. No one will wrap a measuring tape around your skull. You'll usually face a choice of small, medium, or large. Within each group, there will be straps and other devices to fine-tune the fit.

Yet there are a few important guidelines for purchasing the right product. Giro's Richter said that a helmet should be "comfortable but snug. Ideally, what you want from the helmet is, when placed on your head and adjusted to fit, when you move side to side, the skin on your forehead should move with the helmet. Helmets should be in good contact with your head."

The front of the helmet should sit a couple of finger widths above your eyebrow but not interfere with your upper peripheral vision. The sides should extend around and below your ears. The side traps should rest flat or nearly flat against the

Many cyclists will simply look over their helmet after a minor collision and if the plastic isn't cracked, just keep using it. However, they're making a big mistake. In fact, we have been part of several conversations in bike shops where the theory of replacing helmets after accidents was questioned, often with the following sentiment: *Replacing a perfectly good-looking helmet is foolish, it's just a marketing tactic to get you to buy another helmet.*

Not so, says Trek spokesman Eric Bjorling.

"There is no such thing as 'marketing tactics' when lives are at stake," Bjorling said. "Helmets are made, tested, and designed to save lives. But like anything, they weaken after major impact. A lot of the time, the damage is not visible. All of our helmets come with a crash replacement policy so if a rider is in an accident and concerned about their Bontrager helmet, send it back to us for evaluation and we'll send you a new one. Helmets save lives. I speak from personal experience on that."

side of your head. When you buckle the helmet, the straps should "make comfortable contact with your jaw line," Richter said. "You should be able to chew, [but] you don't want to be cutting into your Adam's apple or larynx. I would equate strap fit to the belt on your pants that you don't want so tight that you can't sit down and eat a meal but don't want to be so loose that your pants slide down when you're standing."

5. What's the Best Place to Shop for a Helmet?

Although there are many fine helmets, we'd shop at a bicycle retailer instead of a department store for the same reasons that we buy our bicycle at a bike shop. You'll probably have a better selection of products at a wider range of prices. Sales clerks will know more about products and be able to help you with strap adjustments. You can then make better-informed comparisons for comfort and fit.

You'll want to determine your priorities in purchasing a helmet. If you ride frequently in warm weather and perspire profusely, you'll undoubtedly want something with more venting. This may be more expensive. Creating a helmet that meets strength standards despite having less material requires more sophisticated engineering. If you're a little short in the follicle department, you may want a helmet with more coverage on top to protect you from the sun. "I tell people that helmets are a bit like denim jeans," Richter said. "There are skinny, baggier, boot cuts. Different styles of helmets will cover different amounts of your head. [But] there is a mandatory standard that every helmet in the U.S. must meet."

Try several helmets, the way you test-ride bikes. Look at the fit in a mirror. Shake your head to see if the helmet is tight enough. Ask for help with the straps to ensure that looseness or tightness wasn't simply the result of poor adjustments. Look

Some helmets are ventilated and some are solid.

at the color. We prefer helmets of bright hues. We think that they show up better in traffic and at night. By the way, if you don't find the helmet you want in your size on display, it's okay to take one out of a box.

We happened to be in the market for a helmet as we were researching this book. The straps of our old $25 Bell helmet were no longer tightening to our satisfaction and the extra foam padding had fallen out, leaving exposed pieces of Velcro. We figured we'd buy a low-priced model and tried a $40 black, white, and red Bell Fusion Sport at Orange 20 Bikes in Los Angeles. But the Fusion didn't feel right, and we found it difficult to adjust the straps. We liked the Specialized Echelon better, both for comfort and a flywheel on the back side that allowed us to tighten the helmet with little effort. The Echelon cost $60.

We liked the fit equally of the $55 Giro Rift, which also featured a flywheel. Then because we wanted to see what $100- and $200-plus would buy, we tried a $125 Giro Saro and $225 Specialized S-works helmet. The shell on the latter is built with carbon fiber to allow for increased venting and less weight. We marveled at its lightness.

We looked at helmets at other stores, but their selection was not as large. We returned to Orange 20 to purchase the

Echelon. But we didn't. Here's why. Although according to the Bike Helmet Safety Institute—an Arlington, Virginia, nonprofit, educational group—Specialized is the only major U.S. firm certified to Snell's tougher standards, the Institute expressed reservations about the amount of foam left exposed by the plastic shell. For that reason, and the $5 we saved, we purchased the Rift.

6. Can You Leave a Helmet Outside?

One of the great things about EPS is that it doesn't decompose easily. "It's relatively inert," said Giro's Richter. "Water doesn't bother it. Its performance is consistent through a wide range of temperature changes." Still, he said that EPS may suffer "some degradation" if you leave a helmet in extreme conditions, say hours in the rain or a car trunk that heats to 160 degrees Fahrenheit in summer.

7. Can You Take More Chances with a Helmet?

There is some anecdotal evidence that athletes in high-contact, high-risk activities feel more invulnerable when wearing some of the latest, protective equipment. They hit harder, go faster, or attempt more difficult tricks. This is called risk compensation, and it may lead to injuries. It's difficult to find any indication of risk compensation among the average bike helmet user, and this is as it should be. The helmet is not akin to Hades' Cap of Invisibility, named for the mythological master of the underworld and doffed by Perseus, and assorted larcenous gods, to cloak them from danger. It worked against Medusa but won't do a thing for you if a driver hits you at high speed while you're trying to pass on the right side.

8. How Do You Know That Your Helmet Is Safe? Who Certifies Helmets?

You would be hard-pressed to find a poorly made bicycle helmet at a reputable retailer or big-box store. "If you want a good helmet with good protection, it's easy to find," said Randy Swart, the director of the Bicycle Safety Helmet Institute. "It's hard to find a bad one." Swart's organization is among the country's leading advocates for wearing bike helmets. Its website, Helmets.org, offers an encyclopedic amount of information on helmets, including a yearly analysis of manufacturers and their products.

Look for certification by the Consumer Safety Products Commission. That indicates the helmet has met standards required by federal law. Most bike helmets, certainly those manufactured by Bell, Giro, Specialized, and other leading brands, will bear the CSPC certification mark. Bike helmet companies drop the helmets from 1.2 to 2 meters onto metal anvils at roughly 14 mph. The height and speed of the drop are supposed to emulate a rider's experience. Testing groups also use three different anvils to parallel the angles at which falling riders may hit their heads. Technicians measure the G-force on a central part of a head form on to which the helmet is fixed. A G-force of 300 or more increases the likelihood of a concussion or other head injury and is unacceptable. Better helmets register in the low 100s. You can find a video of the CPSC testing laboratory on the agency's website, or via a link at Helmet.org.

The only caveats are that companies are self-certifying, and there is no comprehensive, all-encompassing compliance program to see if products on store shelves meet CSPC standards. The CSPC does not do the initial testing. A spokesperson said the agency would not comment on whether it tests bike helmets already on the market because it was an "enforce-ment" issue.

A few larger companies have their own laboratories. Most send their helmets to third-party organizations. Is it possible that a defective helmet reaches the market? Huge fines and even jail sentences are supposed to dissuade helmet manu-facturers from marketing defective products. Situations rarely escalate to that level, said Swart. Still, he said that "it's possible that there are helmets out there that don't meet standards," although he added that "if helmets don't meet standards, they're close."

The Snell Institute purchases helmets the same way as consumers and puts them through somewhat more rigorous testing than labs testing for CPSC standards. Snell technicians drop helmets from slightly higher points. Snell is a 54-year-old nonprofit, educational organization. It was named for the racecar driver William "Pete" Snell, who died of head injuries in a crash when his helmet malfunctioned.

Consumer Reports conducts regular tests, but the organiza-tion considers only a small number of helmets. "They're only testing a small sample," said Swart.

You may occasionally find helmets with certification by the American Society for Testing and Materials (ASTM). The ASTM set standards for most of the world's helmets prior to 1999. These standards still exist and are identical to those of the CPSC. But ASTM standards are not U.S. law.

9. What's the Argument Against Helmets?

There are a sizeable number of people worldwide who cycle without helmets. According to a U.S. government National Survey of Bicyclist and Pedestrian Attitudes and Behavior, about one in two cyclists uses a helmet on some trips. All states require children to wear helmets, although the age at which these laws no longer apply varies from under 11 to under 18. Twenty-nine states do not mandate helmets for anyone older than 15.

Those who oppose laws requiring bicycle helmet usage say this:

- The risk of head injury is too small for mandating helmet usage.

- Evidence tying helmets to lower risk of serious head injury is lacking.

- Pro-helmet organizations have failed to present a balanced picture.

- Requiring helmets makes people less likely to cycle.

We think that there is something more basic at work. A lot of people simply don't like being told what to do, even if that thing could save their lives, or the lives of their kids. So they make proposed or possible restrictions an individual rights ruckus. Helmets are a constraint on someone's way of riding. Thirteen states currently have no mandatory helmet law—for kids or adults. These states include Alaska and Arizona, states with a long distrust of laws addressing individual behavior.

We call this group the Venturans, short for former professional wrestler and Minnesota governor Jesse "The Body" Ventura. The buff Ventura won election in the late-1990s partly by loudly promising to veto any state motorcycle helmet law. At the time, a few legislators were threatening to change Minnesota's laissez-faire approach to helmets. The state currently requires anyone 17 and under to wear a motorcycle helmet.

Don't Be a Donorcyclist

Not every cyclist wears a helmet. But before you decide to leave the helmet at home, you may want to listen to what an experienced doctor who has worked in emergency room trauma wards has to say.

"The world needs organ donors too," said Dr. Tim Roberts, M.D. "Many doctors and nurses whom I have worked with over the years have used the term 'donorcycle' to refer to bicyclists or motorcyclists who ride without a helmet. It's such an avoidable accident or death. However, when we find that the person who died from head trauma is an organ donor, we know that something good came out of that cyclist's foolishness."

Roberts' works in Wisconsin where state laws do not require helmets on major roads for bicyclists or motorcyclists over the age of 18. This is despite the fact that both Trek and Harley Davidson are headquartered there.

According to reports from the U.S. Department of Transportation, there were 714 bicycle deaths in 2008. Of those deaths, 91 percent (653) were not wearing a helmet. It is impossible to ignore the statistics.

The American Association of Neurological Surgeons listed bicycling as the No. 1 cause of head injuries that forced a patient to visit an emergency room for treatment or died before treatment was possible in 2009. Of the 446,788 sports-related head injuries reported in 2009, the AANS says that 85,389 (that's 19.1 percent) were from bicycling. How bad is that? Cycling head injuries were just 47 injuries shy of *doubling* the number of head injuries in the No. 2 and No. 3 sports combined (football's 46,948 and baseball/softball's 38,394).

Still think that a major accident cannot happen to you? Then look at one more troubling statistic from the AANS, and you'll see that the trend for more head injuries is not abating. In 2008, the AANS reported that 70,802 cycling head injuries occurred. That is a 20 percent increase in serious head injuries in one year!

"Trauma to the head is a big deal," said Dr. Roberts, who stressed that athletes who pride themselves on having a 'hard head' or dismiss a 'bonk to the head' as being insignificant do not understand what is happening to their brain in an accident. "Cyclists have to remember that a concussion happens because humans have hard skulls. When a cyclist's head is slammed to a stop too quickly what happens is that the brain is then slammed against the very dense bone of the skull. The brain basically floats within the skull, and when either the skull is smashed into the brain or the brain is pushed into the skull, then that contact is what damages the brain and can result in neurological deficits or death."

Non-fatal head injuries can have long-lasting effects.

"There are some things people think are worse than death," Roberts cautioned. "Paralysis, amnesia, loss of speech, and even personality changes are not uncommon for head trauma survivors.

"Riding without a helmet is like playing Russian roulette," Roberts continued. "Not only can it kill you, but you don't know what unique personality trait or desirable brain function you may lose with an injury to the brain. I encourage kids to wear helmets and start when they are on tricycles or Big Wheels to make putting on a helmet a natural part of cycling."

There's a second group who may not all oppose helmet laws but refuses to wear them for stylistic reasons. They believe that helmets belong on lycra-clad century riders. The group is made up of young, male cyclists, often on fixies, who prefer riding as unencumbered as possible. Some of them also don't believe that anything bad can happen to them. A few run-of-the-mill commuters don't like the idea of a glow-in-dark, green Bell with their Brooks Brothers suit. We believe when matched with the right tie or scarf that a helmet makes a strong fashion statement. It says, "I like myself so much that I don't want to wind up speaking with a slur for the rest of my life."

10. Why Don't the Dutch Wear Helmets?

One of the more convincing arguments among people who oppose cycling helmet laws is that the Dutch don't use them much. The Dutch have more bicycles per capita than any other country. They have enough bike lanes that if they were set in one line they would nearly circumnavigate the globe. They even have a special boat for fishing stolen bikes out of Amsterdam's canals. And by the way, the Dutch are not all perfect cycling citizens. In a wacky, largely photographic book, *Bicycle Mania Holland*, we see Dutch cyclists carting too many boxes, carrying passengers where they shouldn't be, and riding on ice. The logic goes that if a country that, warts and all, knows more than anyone else about cycling doesn't see the need for helmets, why should anyone else?

Yet the Bicycle Helmet Institute's Swart, who spent time cycling in Holland a few years ago, said conditions overall there are "much safer." "You'd have to ride in the Netherlands to see how safe it is," he said. "The pedestrians, the cars, and the cyclists all have their own space. The road is always clearly defined. If a car hits a bike, it's always the car's fault."

He said that helmets would be more difficult, even impractical, given the "utilitarian manner" in which the country uses bicycles. "The Dutch use the bike in shopping where they may stop five or six times," he said. "It would be more difficult for them taking the helmets on and off at every stop."

11. How Many Brands Are There? What Are the Prices?

You'll find no shortage of different helmets on the market. Helmets.org, the website of the Bicycle Helmet Safety Institute, lists more than 30 manufacturers, each offering multiple products. Bell, the best-known brand in the U.S., alone sells more than 15 different helmets for children and adults. Bell's models range in cost from $15 to $60. But its high-end Giro division, which sounds Italian but is based in California, offers two models for more than $200 and several others that top $100.

12. Are Expensive Helmets Better Than Cheaper Ones?

The Costco Bell is every bit as likely to protect your pumpkin as a high-end Cratoni (German helmet). The Bicycle Safety Institute proved as much when it tested six helmets a few years ago. All met CSSC standards. The three for less than $20 even bettered those costing more than $150 in impact tests conducted by an independent lab. "If you're concerned about getting the best helmet on the market, you'll have trouble finding out which one that is," said Swart.

When you buy a more costly helmet, you're not paying for more protection but rather for more venting and lighter weight. A Specialized PRO LITE we tried in the course of shopping for a helmet felt as light as a Styrofoam bowl. A salesman said it had more vents than plastic, great for keeping cool, but it wasn't going to keep us safer than Bells costing less than half the price.

Helmets.org lists helmet manufacturers and reviews individual models. It carries the latest news about recalls, safety statistics, and state laws. It also includes a how-to-buy guide.

13. What's Hip in Helmets?

For urban cyclists, a simpler, smoother look has become increasingly popular over the last couple of years. The helmets don't have as many vents and their colors and designs are "more subtle," said Richter. This is the sort of helmet that would look "more reasonable with a suit," he said. "The general style direction is moving to something more organic." Some companies have riffed off this simpler look, adding brims and referencing other types of headwear. The Portland, Oregon–based company Nutcase sells helmets that resemble a beanie and watermelon shell. Another Nutcase helmet sports the British Union Jack. Denmark's Yakkay offers a helmet with five interchangeable tops, all with brims. One cover has a herringbone design, another resembles a bucket hat. The Yakkay helmet sells for $175 at New York retailer Adeline Adeline. The store also sells exquisitely hand-painted helmets by the Human Tarot Project. The helmets, which show images from tarot cards, cost $250.

14. Are Hip Helmets Safe?

We can't vouch for every helmet. But see our comments about Consumer Products Safety Commission and other certifications. If helmets are certified, they meet the standards of the CPSC.

15. Do You Have Any Anecdotes About Helmets Saving a Life?

In 2004, former Olympic cyclist Ron Skarin was riding his usual route from the San Fernando Valley to his West Los Angeles office about 10 miles away. Skarin became a building

Psychedelic Nutcase helmet. (J. MAUS/BIKEPORTLAND)

inspector for Los Angeles in his postathletic career. It was 6:30 on a clear, dark morning—so dark he hadn't switched off his bike's taillights. Traffic was light on the last flat part of the trip when he felt his front tire dragging. He was riding about 20 mph, an easy speed for him. Skarin tried "hopping" the front wheel to see if it had gone flat. The next thing he remembers was waking up in his bedroom a week later. Skarin's tire had dislodged from the front fork, and he'd fallen headfirst. A passing motorist saw him in a heap and called the paramedics. The impact had shattered his helmet and left him in a twilight zone. He still doesn't recall what happened during the ensuing week. "I had a pretty severe concussion," Skarin said. "Apparently, I was never totally unconscious, but I had amnesia."

That was with wearing a helmet!

5

Accessories

You May Not Think You Need Them
but You Should Make Sure You Have Them

You have your bike. You have a helmet that fits right. A rear rack. Clothes that feel comfortable.

Now what?

It's time to accessorize.

Accessories fit into two categories: those you need or are better to have around than not and those that are kind of fun to have around.

When you buy a bicycle, you should budget for the first category, particularly lights and reflectors. At some point you'll be riding when it's dark, and you'll need lights to see the road. More importantly, you'll need both to be seen by drivers, not to mention cyclists and pedestrians. Lights and reflectors are part of being a responsible cyclist. Tool kits are helpful. Fenders can help keep water and dirt off your pants. We'll add a good saddle to the mix. The saddles on bikes often don't feel right. Sitting comfortably is essential for ensuring that you want to cycle.

The rest of the stuff that'll we'll discuss here is for discretionary spending. You don't need bells, decorations, kickstands, or a good water bottle to cycle anymore than you need baskets or bags. People have cycled for decades without any of these things.

On the other hand, cycling is inherently personal. Whatever you do to make your bicycle your own can only enhance your experience. Whether it's riding a fixie with skulls or adding a bell you don't need to the handlebars, if it's something you can be proud of, you'll want to ride more.

That's the idea.

Reflectors

Most bicycles these days come with reflectors. That's as it should be. Reflectors are part of a solid defense system for riding in fading light and dark. They reflect the beams of headlights, enabling drivers to see you. The most effective and commonly placed reflectors are under the saddle, on pedals, and in the spokes. The reflector under the saddle is about the same height as headlights. The unsynchronized movement of the reflectors on the pedals and spokes is more likely to catch a driver's eye than stationary reflectors. Red reflectors are more effective than the white or clear variety.

Some bikes can be short of reflectors, or may not have enough to satisfy your safety urges. Our 10-year-old Specialized Rockhopper lacks a reflector under the saddle. You can buy extras in stores or online. A circular reflector with bracket sold on Amazon.com costs $2.50. We found others that could be mounted under seats or on rear racks for $2 to $4 more than that, and a yellow spokes reflector for $10.

Reflecting tape you add to your clothing or helmet can be even more effective, particularly if you're creative in your patterning.

San Francisco-based Betabrand also manufactures a line of five-pocket, cotton twill Bike to Work pants—perfect for office casual days. Turn the cuffs and rear pockets inside out to reveal blue-checked, reflective material. The pants are available in five colors and cost $90.

Yet reflectors are no substitute for good lights.

Let us repeat: reflectors are no substitute for lights. The cycling website SheldonBrown.com—named for the late West Newton, Massachusetts, bike mechanic—outlines reflectors' limitations.

- Reflectors may not catch a car's headlights.

- The narrow beam of reflected light may not catch the driver's eye.

- If reflectors are poorly installed, or knocked out of place, they may point in a less optimal direction.

- Grit, scuffing, and scratches can impair reflectors' effectiveness.

- Not all cars have two working headlights.

Lights

Lights are essential if you're going to do any night riding. They are the most effective way of ensuring that drivers see you. A headlight mounted on the handlebars or just below is well situated for catching drivers' attention. We've heard of experienced cyclists recommending two headlights, one pointed down to help identify potential hazards and the second straight ahead to alert oncoming traffic. Tail lights, flashing or otherwise,

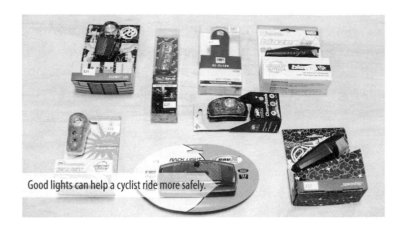
Good lights can help a cyclist ride more safely.

Eye See Your Point

You don't have to be an ophthalmologist to understand the need for decent eyewear when bicycling. After all, the easiest way to find yourself in an accident is to not see where you are going. If you mount your bike without eye protection, you are asking for a life-altering moment. Or maybe it should be called a life-ending moment because just a fleck of dirt or dust flying into your unprotected eye can lead to catastrophe.

One of the authors learned that the hard way thousands of miles ago. When he first began riding daily, wearing eye protection didn't seem vital. An early winter chill sent a light dusting of snow flurries that weren't heavy enough to accumulate on the streets. But riding at 15 mph, we had a snowflake fly directly into one eye while crossing a major intersection. Unexpectedly blinded, we were able to steer quickly to the side of the road and rub the flakes away, but it was sheer luck that a passing car didn't hit us when the shock of being suddenly blinded made us.

Since that day, we have not jumped on a bike without eye protection. You do not have to be fastidious about your eyewear. In fact, after having paid $60 for a pair of multilens cycling glasses, we decided that there was no point in paying good money for glasses. Expensive multilens glasses are not practical. Do you want to track extra lenses and switch lenses based on sunlight levels? After months of switching the lenses, we found that the glasses had stretched, the lenses were no can help protect you from behind. Many lights do not require tools to install. The lighting mounts clip on or fit snugly over handlebars and tubes.

You can buy a battery-operated light that in some cases is rechargeable. Rechargeable batteries are lead, nickel cadmium, or nickel metal hydride. Lead batteries are cheaper. But they are also heavier and may die if unused. NiCad and NiMH batteries should be drained and recharged to have a longer life. Yet cyclists complain that the light from these batteries can die quickly. Prices range from under $20 to more than $450. A Bell Sports Night Trail Light system with headlight and rear light costs just $13 but won almost unanimous kudos from consumers rating it on a Walmart website. The lights take normal batteries. An REI headlight and tail light combination costs nearly six times that. A Niterider Minewt with rechargeable battery is more than double the price of the REI product.

longer staying put, and they had grown scratched from manhandling. And when you lose one lens—and you *will* lose a lens if you use them for any time—what good are fancy, expensive glasses?

Our suggestion: buy $10 drugstore glasses and don't worry if they break.

However, Christina Curas with the American Academy of Ophthalmology cautions that getting the right glasses for the right sport is more important than what shades look good with your new haircut.

"It is true that protective eyewear is very important for any sport that you may be playing or participating in," Curas said. "Ninety percent of eye injuries could be prevented by wearing proper eye protection. But it is very important that you wear the proper eyewear for your sport with the correct lens."

The American Society for Testing and Materials sets standards for eye-safety standards, according to Curas. More information about preventing eye injury in sports can be found at the AAO's helpful site, www.geteyesmart.org.

Some cyclists also opt for old-fashioned headlamps that fit tightly over helmets via a strong elastic band. You can find headlamps for under $20, although we spied a Niterider Pro 600 on sale for just under $500. The Pro 600 includes software for calibrating brightness and duration of the light.

Your Tool Kit

You should prepare a tool kit with enough gear to rescue you from flat tires and other common maladies that you can fix on

Sunglass Techno-speak Translated

Whether you decide to buy the expensive pair of Oakleys that "look cool" or a cheaper pair of throwaways, knowing what characteristics the sunglasses possess will help you decide what to purchase.

Today's top-shelf sunglasses can have so much technology involved in their creation that the average person has no idea if a pair of UV-protected, photochromatic glasses are better than a pair of mirrored, polarized ones. To help you, we've defined sunglass features below.

Tinting

The color of the glasses determines the elements of the light spectrum that will be absorbed. It will change how you see the world. Different tinted glasses are better for different sports.

Grey: The most popular color, grey, reduces brightness and glare and offers you the best chance to see colors. Grey lenses are the best option for cyclists. Keep a pair in your backpack.

Yellow/orange: These lenses emphasize contrast in low-light or hazy conditions, making objects appear sharper and easier to see. For cyclists: on rides at dawn and dusk, or in hazy conditions, a pair of yellow or orange glasses may prove better. But be prepared to switch to grey lenses if the sun starts to shine brighter.

Green: Green lenses can reduce eye strain in bright conditions by filtering some of the blue light spectrum. These lenses usually offer more contrast and sharpness; they are basically a combination of the grey and yellow/orange lenses. You may find that one pair of green glasses can the spot. You'll be more apt to continue cycling if you can tend to your bike instead of having to bring it to the local shop. Such visits involve time and waiting and may interfere with your returning to the road. Remove the obstacle. Prepare your tool kit and carry it with you on trips of any length. Most serious riders we know pack their kit in their backpack or bag. But if you'd like to go retro, a number of companies produce tool bags that fit under your saddle and will even accommodate today's smaller pumps.

replace both a pair of grey and yellow/orange lenses. But you won't know unless you can try them in bright and cloudy situations.

Brown/amber: By blocking out blue light, these glasses are designed to give you better clarity and contrast in darker conditions and are best used when looking into green (pastures) or blue (sky) backgrounds.

Red: Like the others, these block blue light to increase contrast. The rose color is often cited as being more soothing. See what you think when looking into sunlight. Does everything become one rosy color, or are you able to clearly see contrast between objects?

Other Lens Treatments

Polarization: Whether it's natural or man-made, light vibrates and radiates in all directions. Light that is reflected, scattered, refracted, or transmitted from direct light creates many planes of light waves that cause glare (look out any window on a sunny day and notice the countless directions from which the sun is bouncing off surfaces). Reducing the amount of light waves reduces glare, especially light waves that are on a horizontal axis. Polarized lenses create an artificial barrier to reduce light waves penetrating the sunglasses so that only sunlight coming from a specific plane is allowed through. Typically, polarized glasses will block glare from such horizontal surfaces as lakes, puddles, and car hoods while allowing vertical light waves to penetrate. To see the polarization in effect, take a pair of glasses and hold them so you can look through one lens and turn to look at a shiny horizontal surface. The light should be hard

continued on next page

Pumps

You should have a pump. You'll have options. Smaller pumps with a detachable attachment are serviceable and pack easily. We fit one pump in an eyeglasses case—really. However, small pumps take longer to fill tires. If you want something that can generate a larger volume of air but don't want the hassle of packing a pump separately from your tool bag, you can opt for an old-style frame-mounted pump. Schwinn manufactures an $8 aluminum pump that would have looked at home on a 1970s 10-speed model. Topeak produces a $50 carbon fiber model. Most frame pumps cost between $12 and $25. Zefal, Blackburn, and Planet Bike Roadie are among other prominent pump manufacturers. Assembling the mount usually doesn't take more than a few minutes.

to look at with your naked eye, but when you look through the polarized lens the surface should be clear.

Photochromatic (also known as "photochromic"): Invented in the 1960s, these lenses will darken when exposed to sunlight and return to their normal nondarkened state when the glasses are out of direct sunlight. Wearers should be warned that this technology is rendered useless if they are behind windows that block UV light, which most car windows and some industrial or home windows do. Because the window blocks UV light, that means there is so little UV light remaining that the glasses may not darken or only slightly. (Hint: you also may want to consult your significant other before purchasing sunglasses with these lenses as many people refer to these as "old-man glasses." We want to help you survive socially as well as physically!)

Mirroring: Aside from hiding who you are really looking at, mirrored glasses have a practical function, thanks to a special coating called a "half-silvered surface." This coating allows for half the incoming light to be reflected away so that it is easier to see in bright conditions. This thin surface is susceptible to scratching however so be careful handling these sunglasses.

Fender Guards

Some people think fender guards are nerdy. We find them practical. They will protect your clothing, particularly when the ground is wet and filled with puddles. You can buy fenders in plastic, chrome, aluminum, and

Fenders

even wood. There are also synthetic clip-on and inflatable fenders. Unless heavily varnished and maintained, wooden fenders aren't the most practical selection, although they garner style points. You can purchase serviceable fenders for your front and rear tires for under $50. Topeak, Schwinn, Sks, Zefal, and Planet Bike are among leading fender manufacturers. Couple fenders with mud flaps for extra protection.

Scratch-resistant: Glass may be scratch-resistant, but plastic and other compounds used to make most sunglasses are not. To protect sunglasses made of plastic, a thin film made of polycrystalline diamond or diamond-like carbon is used to make this hardy layer that prevents most scratches, but not all.

Anti-reflection: Designed to reduce glare, antireflection coating is a thin film layered on the front and back of the lens to reduce what is called "back glare," or the light that hits the back of the lenses and enters the eyes.

UV coating: This simple layer added to sunglasses should be a part of any pair of glasses you buy. There are two types of ultraviolet light, and one of them (UV-B) is not a concern for most adults because the cornea absorbs all UV-B light. However, the other form of UV light is called UV-A. Extended exposure to UV-A causes cataracts, blindness, cancer of the eye, and other unpleasant outcomes. Look for glasses that block 100 percent of UV radiation. A tag on the glasses should indicate if they block UV-A, UV-B, or both and the percentage. You want to block 100 percent of all UV light.

Bells

We have fond memories of bells on the handlebars of our first bikes. They made a pleasing ringing sound. And by using them, we had the feeling for one of the first times in our young lives that we were dictating terms to adults. Our ring meant they had to get out of the way. Our kids had bells on their first bikes and seemed to feel the same way.

But bells are practical. They let people in front of you know that you're coming through—and with little more than a nudge from your finger. The flip side is that if you have an overly heavy trigger finger, you risk annoying other people. Most of the bells we looked at cost less than $10 and seemed easy to install. You fit the bell's mount over the handlebars, same as in the old days. The bells themselves haven't changed much. They are circular with a sort of trigger extending out, like the tongue of a clam. Some companies employ a translucent housing to reveal the inner workings of the bell. Others have painted designs or slogans on the covering.

You can find many different bells in retail shops.

Kickstands

We have nothing against kickstands. We just don't have one, at least since the one we purchased loosened. We kept retightening it and it kept loosening until we grew fed up and removed it. That was several years ago, and we haven't missed it. In cities there are so many places against which to lean a bicycle. The important thing in buying a kickstand is to ensure that it's the right size. Different frames require a different length. And if you're going to make a mistake, then it's better to cut too little than too much—same as with pants. That's because if you cut too much, you can't add back inches. If you cut too little, there's still room for adjustment. You can find an adequate kickstand for under $10. Two-legged kickstands provide more stability. But they are also more expensive and may not be in retailers' stock. You'll have an easier time finding one of these online.

Seats

We hesitate to call a bicycle saddle an accessory. Saddles are vitally important. A comfortable saddle may be the difference between an enjoyable or unenjoyable riding experience. That's understandable given that you're spending most of your time on your rear. The saddle that comes with the bike you purchase may not be the right one for you. Try it out. Then try another and another, until you find one that feels right. Good shops will let you test-drive saddles. They're fine switching them out. The one you reject may be perfect for someone else.

Saddles may be made of synthetic materials and cushioned. Or they may be of hard leather. Some have long noses—the forward point of the saddle—others are more snubbed. There are also seats without noses, although some people say that it's difficult to balance and control a bike from this sort of perch.

Bicycle seats come in various shapes and sizes.

We haven't had the opportunity to test one. Cushioned seats are often less comfortable than the hardened leather variety.

Our neighbor Matthew Butterick swears by the narrow British-manufactured Brooks leather saddle that he bought in 2009 when he grew uncomfortable with the original saddle on his hybrid. Some Brooks saddles cost more than $350. They are made of leather with steel—or in a few cases, titanium—undercarriages. The thickness of the leather may vary.

Brooks has roots in the late nineteenth century, when its founder, John Boultbee Brooks, patented his first saddle. His invention was an improvement over other seats at the time. Brooks makes saddles for, among others, women and people with larger inner thighs. Brooks saddles take breaking in, sometimes a couple hundred miles worth. They also require extra care. Saddle soap or beeswax can help protect the leather against rain.

Water Bottles

You can still purchase a water bottle and cage for the bottom tube. Most of these are under $20 and easy to mount. The bottles are made of plastic, steel, or aluminum and hold about a quart of liquid. Regardless of the material, clean them out regularly with dish soap or throw the nonaluminum ones into your dish washer. (Dish washing detergent is hard on aluminum.)

Computers

We don't much care how fast we're going or how many miles we've ridden. But we understand those who feel strongly about analyzing everything. For them, there is an array of gadgets for recording data. Simple computers will tell you your speed and mileage. The most sophisticated and expensive computers will provide much, much more than that. A $650 Polar CS600X will track your cumulative ascents and descents, barometer, heart rate, and calorie consumption. It will tell you when you are no longer riding in your target heart rate and keep a weekly review of your cycling sessions. Of course, this is all much more than the average cyclist will need. But it's there if you want it.

Smartphone Applications

Over the past few years, smartphones such as the iPhone and devices running Google's Android operating system have gone from niche to mainstream. As these devices pack high-speed data connections, accelerometers, and GPS chips onboard, several bicycling-related apps for these phones have recently come to market. Nothing against technology, but bike applications are not indispensable. You don't need to know your speed for a commute or grocery run. Moreover, we find applications a little counter to the back-to-basics spirit of urban cycling. People cycled joyfully for the 150 years prior to the iPhone. We could argue that smartphones are even a detriment, a distraction for the occasional cyclist trying to multitask.

Yet we will not deny that a few applications are handy and may even help you ride safer. Consider Brakelights, which transforms a smartphone into a brightly lit brake light—a major assistance if your usual brake light fails after dark or if, heaven forbid, you don't have a brake light. Download the $1 application and attach it to your clothing, a rear rack, basket,

Nuts and Bolts of Going Noseless

Medical science appears to have proven what many male cyclists have known for years—traditional bike seats just aren't good for you. Worse yet, the long, narrow seats that most adults grew up riding may be bad for a guy.

At the time of Y2K, noseless saddles were a rarity. Back then, a cyclist looking to shorten his seat would need a hacksaw and lots of duct tape. Today, however, there are many manufacturers of noseless saddles and a surprising variety. ECD, Ergo, Hobson, ISM, and Schwinn are just some of the manufacturers of no-pressure saddles.

About 3,000 miles ago, one of the authors switched from a traditional bike seat to a noseless one. The only regret: not switching sooner. Removing the long nose at the front of the seat is such a major relief that we would urge any man who commutes, is considering commuting, or plans any long-distance riding to switch. If our real-world experience isn't good enough, just ask the Center for Disease Control.

"The traditional bicycle saddle has a narrow nose or horn that protrudes under the groin as the cyclist straddles the bicycle," the CDC explains on its site. "Ideally, the weight of the cyclist supported on the saddle should be under the pelvic sit bones. However, 25 percent or more of the body weight is supported where the groin contacts the saddle nose. This percentage greatly increases as the cyclist leans forward in more aerodynamic positions. Bearing weight on this region of the saddle compresses the nerves and arteries in the groin. These nerves and arteries run through the groin between the sit bones to the genitals. Research has shown that pressure on these nerves and arteries over time may lead to a loss of sensation and a decrease in blood supply to the genitals. This can contribute to the sexual and reproductive health effects that have been reported with bicycling."

We should note here that some riders have said that they find a noseless seat awkward at first and even report that they have less control of the bike. Like most new things, it will take time to get used to a noseless seat. After trying one, you may find it too unusual to use every day. Or, like many riders, you may wonder why you didn't try it sooner. There are no completely right or wrong answers.

What are the best noseless seats? The following is our review of four that are the most common in the U.S. (ECD is sold largely in the United Kingdom.):

ISM Touring Saddle

This was one of our favorite noseless saddles. The only reason we say "was" and not "is" is because other cyclists apparently liked the seat, too. It was stolen in late 2010 from in front of our condo. The ISM tends to feel more like sitting on a bench than a seat, which is preferred. However, the

ISM's Touring saddle. (COURTESY OF IDEAL SEAT MODIFICATION)

solid stitching around the top has a tendency to wear straight grooves into your body right where your upper thigh becomes the buttocks, especially when leaning forward for extended periods. We would prefer that the seat had a more curved edge as the flat top and ninety-degree edges where the side and top meet left us rubbing our butt often after a ride.

Ergo Endurance

This seat is easily the best of the ones we have ridden. The rounded edges on the Ergo fix all the problems that the ISM has. Not only does the Ergo reduce groin pressure, but there are no awkward or annoying stiff edges to constantly wear against your hamstrings or glutes.

Ergo's Endurance saddle. (COURTESY OF ERGO, LLC)

Hobson Easyseat / Easyseat II

We love the creativity of the design because it is so ergonomically designed that it has to be great, right? However, it is not. While it is definitely an improvement over traditional seats, the pitch of the seat is so steep that you end up riding standing up and only lean back against the

Hobson's Easyseat II. (COURTESY OF HOBSON ASSOCIATES, INC., LLC)

seat at stoplights. You never fully sit because the upright angle of the seat doesn't tilt backward much. Inventor Rich Hobson told us that he had heard that complaint before, so he created the Easyseat II. However, taking the Easyseat II on test rides didn't reveal much difference. The Hobson is better than a normal seat, but definitely be prepared to ride "messenger style"—standing up the majority of the time. One major plus is the kidney-shaped pads that are comfortable and do not wear on the glutes or hamstrings.

Schwinn No Pressure

Costing about one-third of what the other seats will run you, Schwinn's No Pressure saddle is a great deal for the money. However, it is not the best seat. The wide platform is comfortable but feels more like sitting on a park bench. If your rides are around the neighborhood, this is your seat.

Schwinn's No Pressure saddle. (COURTESY OF SCHWINN)

But if you're looking for a long-term answer you are better off paying $20 more and getting either the ISM or the Ergo designs.

or pannier. The accelerometer determines when you slow, triggering the phone screen to flash red. The Back Light offers a similar safety benefit, with a twist. Back Light turns your phone into an effective light but can also transmit short messages to traffic. "Back off," "Slow down," and "Stay clear" are a few directions that come to mind. But we could imagine some wittier, if not more pungent, options.

We've read praise for the Gear Calculator. But we have few doubts that the kind words came from more wonkish riders. Gear Calculator calculates gear ratios based on crank lengths and wheel and sprocket sizes—in English, what gear you should use for optimal riding. The application can also help you minimize tire wear. Of course, we favor the less sophisticated trial-and-error approach. We've found that a handful of rides or so will usually tell you what works best.

The Bike Computer turns your smartphone into a dashboard. It records current, maximum, and average mph, time traveled, and it saves trip information. But we've read mixed reviews about its reliability and the developer's responsiveness to customer complaints. Remember that bike applications are like any product or service. Shop wisely before you buy. The Cycle Meter records speed, distance traveled, and trip time—albeit via a garish interface filled with green and orange. BikePRO advertises itself as a low-cost cycling computer. It logs the date, duration, distance, and average speed of every trip and allows for entries on weather and other details. Ride the City will help cyclists find the safest and shortest routes in 26 cities worldwide.

We've found applications to help monitor personal fitness, find the latest news on particular bike brands, and solve repair problems. Yet the best use of the smartphone may be as a GPS navigation device for directions or to check weather and traffic reports.

6

Clothes

How to Survive by Wearing the Right Things

We want you to look great on your cycle.

But when it comes to cycling clothing and accessories, there's no right way. We repeat.

There is no right way.

Cycling is the supreme individualist's sport. You ride the way you want to ride. You ride who you are. That self-expression depends on your age, your budget, and most of all what image you want to project—or not. It all manifests itself in basic decisions about the type of bike you ride, whether to wear a helmet or not, how to carry your stuff, and, of course, haberdashery.

Are you looking to unleash your inner pro rider? We'll look for your skin-tight, Cocona polymer shorts and shirts in colors fit for a clown parade, coupled with ultralight, carbon composite cycling shoes.

Cycling shoes come in many different styles.

Cocona is short for coconut carbon. Really.

Do you like bike gear with less polish? Try the Oakley cargo-mountain-bike shorts with an REI-moisture-wicking Night Prowler T-shirt. The shorts and shirt say that you like comfort and convenience, particularly with pockets for carrying your flotsam and jetsam, but that you don't want to be too obvious. Pearl Izumi has a nice plaid number you could wear at a '60s-themed pool party.

You could string together outfits of sweats, old shorts, windbreakers, and other decidedly non-bicycle-specific gear to say you don't care what people think of your attire. Try stripes with checks, plaids with polka-dots, high-top Cons, and a bright neckerchief you can pull over your mouth on high-pollution days. Or you could just go business casual, or in a full-fledged suit. You can even bike in high heels.

If you wore a suit, you'd be cycling European commuter style. Urban bicycling Europeans don't bother with special clothing. They wear whatever they are going to wear for the rest of the day.

The French have the most élan. No one looks as elegant on a bicycle as Parisians commuting around the Eiffel Tower on a "Velibe". These bikes are part of the city's metro system—short-term rental bikes that Paris (also Brussels, Milan, and other cities) started providing in 2007 to reduce traffic. The bikes are industrial strength, heavy and awkward to maneuver. You slip the Velibe's front wheel into an electromagnetic port when you're done riding, and it stays there until the next rider activates the release. Ridden by a Parisian woman in a flowing skirt and heels, or an impeccably coiffed man, the Velibe assumes new dimensions. Suits barely wrinkle. Shoes glimmer. Scarves flow in the breeze. The average Paris Velibist could be picking up groceries or on her way to a formal dinner, and you'd never tell the difference by dress alone. A baguette and flowers in a front basket are usually the telltale signs she's eating in.

"You don't need all sorts of cycling gear," said Julie Hirschfeld, the founder of Adeline Adeline, a New York City bike retailer specializing in three- and eight-speed city bikes and accessories. "If you go to Amsterdam, people are just riding. They have a rain poncho. They get out and go. A lot of people who ride are hyped by gear. But the casual city cyclist doesn't need to get anything special."

Hirschfeld commutes three miles over the Brooklyn Bridge on a city bike, in colder weather wearing a favorite pair of fleece-lined APC wedges, in a dress or work slacks. She carries her work items in a Basil bottle basket-rear rack combo so she doesn't have to wear a backpack, which makes her perspire. About Hirschfeld's only real bike gear item is a fleece-lined helmet. "I preach simplicity," she said.

In the interest of proving a point and to see if we could spot some overriding urban bike clothing trend, we decided to take a closer look at what people are wearing. We spoke with urban cyclists around the country and looked at sales racks in stores. We spent time watching cyclists in Los Angeles, which is simultaneously the butt of fashion jokes and setter of fashion trends. Just for fun we also decided to see what sort of outfit we could buy for an obscene amount of money. We'll start there, with a section we'll call…

You Spent What on an Outfit?

It's no secret that many cyclists love gear. It is also no secret that many companies have sprouted in recent years to fan this love affair. They are manufacturing new types of gear crafted of materials with names that sound as if they could be part of the space shuttle. We've sometimes wondered what all the fuss is about. We were fine with the wicking abilities of a good cotton shirt or light wool overshirt.

We recently saw an article on the world's most expensive bikini. It was made of 15 karats of flawless diamonds and cost $30 million. Model Molly Sims was quite the hit when she—barely—donned it for the *Sports Illustrated* swimsuit issue. We do not foresee anything similar for cyclists but that isn't to say that you can't spend more than $1,000—as much as a good business suit—on a cycling outfit. What do you get for that amount? Here's one vision.

We started with a Pearl Izumi Octane Bib short. We have no idea why anyone would want to ride anywhere in something called a bib, or a garment that looks like something you'd find on a Victorian schoolboy. These shorts loop over your shoulders like a tank-top undershirt. The front has been scooped out to just above the belly button. The shorts are made of something called P.R.O. Transfer Fabric, which keeps you dry while you're sweating by absorbing your perspiration and wicking it outside. Most high-end bike materials do the same. Who has the best system these days? It depends on whose marketing department you believe.

Bicyclists in Portland participate in a "Tweed Ride," proving that almost any attire can work on a bicycle. (J. MAUS/BIKEPORTLAND)

The bib has an anatomical fit—too anatomical in some areas for our taste. But it will show off your bulging pectorals and biceps. We suppose that gives it an intimidation factor, particularly if you wear it without a shirt. What person would want to mess with a muscular bicyclist wearing a bib? You would have to assume such an aggressor is either crazy or a professional wrestler.

The bib has a multipanel design, meaning that it has combined different pieces of fabric. Higher-end bike shorts combine panels instead of using one or two sections of cloth. The multipanels can be stitched together so that the shorts bend the way you do. This feature is supposed to make the shorts last longer. The bib has 4D chamois for cushioning around the seat (chamois is the material of choice for padding) and is handmade in Italy, the capital of fine clothing production. What more could you ask for?

We'll combine our Octane Bib with a $225 Octane full-zip jersey. The Octane jersey has, of course, the best in Italian styling, wicking material, and venting to help keep you cool on hot days. It has P.R.O. antimicrobial material under the armpits to stifle odors stemming from all the hard riding you'll be doing, and it somehow manages to include three pockets on the back of the shirt, plus a waterproof zip pocket. We assume the waterproof pocket is where you'll be stuffing your pens and paper. But what we like best are the elasticized gripper, which keeps the shirt hem in place, and full-length front zipper. Pull the front zipper halfway down, and you will exude ruggedness.

You'll need gloves, and Pearl Izumi has a bunch of those. Spend $35 for the P.R.O. leather Pittards. They have a carbon leather palm and mesh venting that cools but simultaneously provides protection against the sun. We appreciate attending job interviews without sweaty, sunburned hands.

In our fictional spend-at-will-on-bike-stuff shopping trip, we'll put you in Pearl Izumi Octane shoes. They're light and provide lots of pedaling power. But they only cost $300. There are far more expensive shoes for sale. Let's go for the $550 Sidi Ergo II, designed for Italian professional cyclist Paolo Bettini. They are also very light and have a super-hardened sole to enhance cycling power. The gold trim represents Bettini's gold medal in the 2004 Athens Olympics' road race. What makes the Ergo II worth $150 more than the Pearl Izumi shoes? We don't know, but we're confident if you wear a pair, you'll be early to meetings.

By the way, you can get a good pair of wool cycling socks for another $20.

Total cost of our outfit: $1,120. That doesn't include the helmet.

You'll arrive at your office sleek and dry.

But the question will be how you're going to untangle yourself from the bib.

Bike Clothes…but Not Overdoing It

This is what we call the middle road. You can wear bicycle clothes that don't cost a fortune, match pants to shirt, or look particularly cool. You can mix these items with workout clothes or old clothes you don't care much about. This may be the best option for people who worry about sweating through their civilian attire.

Former Olympian Ron Skarin preferred cycling clothes when he commuted years ago to his job as a Los Angeles building inspector. Skarin, who retired in 2010, had access to the latest cycling materials but wore simple, inexpensive outfits. He kept changes of work clothes at the office and rinsed off at a bathroom sink.

Boston cyclist Mark Halliday wears simple cycling shorts with cotton shirts in temperate weather. In winter, he dresses in layers: fleece pants under an unpadded pair of Pearl Izumi shorts, long-sleeved shirts, wool socks, a vest, and a windbreaker. He'll top it with a headband to cover his ears, and on the most severe days, he'll also wear a facemask, along with ski gloves and zip booties over his Shimano clip-on shoes. And he'll always have a waterproof Gortex

Dressing in layers helps a cyclist pedal on through the winter months. (J. MAUS/BIKEPORTLAND)

Never Buy Black

"Well, cyclists think they're fashionable, too, I guess?"

My cycling friend's sheepish reply was more comical than informative, but it was the best answer to one of the most vexing questions in cycling apparel: why is so much designed in black?

When buying cycling gear—hat, gloves, balaclava, neck gaiter, leg gaiters, socks, shoes, shirts, shorts, leg warmers, sunglasses, jackets, etc.—any color *except* black.

Black is a "slimming" tone for us, ahem, large people. The same theory also makes small black objects disappear when stuffed into a backpack, pannier, shelf, or closet.

It becomes nearly impossible to find a missing glove or neck gaiter in a backpack filled with gear when all the gear is black.

For example, recently a fellow cyclist was asking about different flashlights. We had the perfect small flashlight to show her, but when we went home and looked through our cycling gadgets bag, we couldn't find it. It was only after sifting through the objects that we found that, indeed, the flashlight had been right there the whole time. But it was coated in black plastic, which made it nearly invisible against the dark interior of the bag.

At cycling stores, compare how quickly you notice neon green jackets compared to black ones. Do the same for other items—dark colors become obscured and blend while bright ones stand out.

Having a hard time locating the bright-colored clothing? Try looking in the clearance bin. We're serious! The one thing that can prevent many moments of needless frustration is often ignored, even shunned, by cyclists—the color of their clothing.

Bright clothing can help drivers see you, too, though you should not rely on it. The best way to avoid an accident is to cycle predictably on city streets, not run red lights, and refrain from doing foolish things like making a left-hand turn from the right lane. Your clothing selection won't matter if you ride like an idiot.

shell and pants available for unexpected rains. He carries his work clothes on the back of his bike and showers and changes at the office. "I've been out in zero degrees," Halliday said. "People think I'm crazy, but you would be surprised how quickly you warm up."

Protecting Your Trousers, er, Pants

One of the traditional dangers of riding in civies is loose pant legs. They get caught in chains. They get dirty. Today's Mad Men–inspired, narrow styles are less susceptible to damage. But if you want to lessen the risk of ruining a good pair of work slacks, you'll roll up your pant legs or buy a clip. The former summons thoughts of an English schoolmaster protecting his tweeds. One pant leg up and one down has a nerdy cool. Pants-rollers face two decisions: whether to roll inward or outward, and how far to roll. We prefer the outward roll. It's easier than the inward roll to execute quickly and less likely to unfurl. The downside of the outward roll is that it leaves more pronounced wrinkles. Call this accordion leg. Accordion leg is not the worst possible style error, and it may be mitigated somewhat by the increased use of wrinkle-free fabrics. On the other hand, accordion leg draws the sort of unwanted notice no one wants before a big meeting. As for the amount of roll-up, we recommend a hearty three or four folds. An alternative to the roll-up is the vertical-fold, tuck-your-pants-in-your-socks approach. Grab the crease and fold gently inward. Then tuck the pants leg in your socks.

Straps and clips secured by small buckles, Velcro, and other closing mechanisms offer yet another option. You wrap them around your lower calf. They may leave a crease. Your pants will also still be vulnerable to grit and grease kicking off the road and chain. Yet we admired a stylish leather-covered, steel, spring-loaded trouser clip by saddle manufacturer Brooks. The Brooks clip operates along the same line as a carpenter's metal measuring tape. It wraps easily around a lower leg yet has the firmness to hold in check a flapping cuff without leaving too many creases. Combine the trouser clip with a retro chain and fender guards, and you'll be more likely to arrive at your destination with clean, smooth pants.

You Could Do Nothing Special at All

Kelly Martin commutes to her job in Los Angeles as director of the co-op Bike Kitchen in stylish, lace-up ankle boots, office-ready pants, and blouse. Bike Kitchen volunteers Jonathan West and Joe Skala wear jeans, athletic or casual shoes, and pullovers. If veteran urban cyclists don't feel the need to wear cycling clothes, and they ride more than 20 miles on some days, why should anyone else—unless you have particularly active sweat glands?

One midevening in midwinter, we were gazing at nighttime bicycle traffic on one of Los Angeles' most significant bike lanes downtown—Sunset Boulevard. Cycling traffic was light.

At one point, we spied a cyclist on a hybrid headed west from the city. It was cold by Southern California standards, a little breezy, and damp. Los Angeles in winter always has a few weeks of steady rain. The cyclist wore a white helmet, a windbreaker/rain jacket with reflectors, sensible shoes, and pants with metal clips to keep his hem from getting stuck in the chain. He carried his belongings in rear panniers. Nothing he wore would have landed him in *Esquire*'s pages. Windbreakers are functional, not stylish.

Still, the rider looked comfortable and professional in the way he progressed through the hip Silver Lake section. We imagined that he was a longtime commuter who'd learned exactly how to outfit himself and his bike for any conditions.

We thought this cyclist looked great.

Others would differ.

That's the best thing about bike fashion.

You don't need anything special.

You wear what you want.

Then you just go.

7

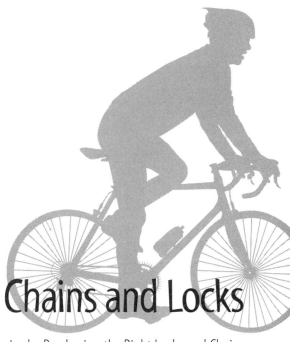

Chains and Locks

How to Survive by Purchasing the Right Locks and Chains

It was once safe to be a two-wheeled vehicle.

The times were gentler, except for the occasional civil war or foreign colonization, and a so-called mechanical horse through its earliest iterations was not the most coveted item. No one knew what to make of velocipedes. Only masochists would have wanted a boneshaker. As for high-wheelers, how would someone have gotten away with stealing one? *Hey, you up there, that's my bike!*

While we do not know of any comprehensive chronicle of bike theft, we suppose that shortly after early modern bicycles appeared in the nineteenth century that someone stole one. It had to have happened at some point. It's the dark side of human nature to take something that looks good. Maybe there's a record in a dusty Boston or Philadelphia police blog.

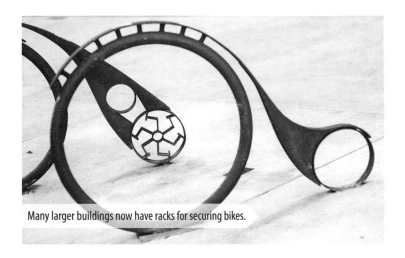

Many larger buildings now have racks for securing bikes.

We think the odds are that the thefts occurred in a big city. More people means more temptation. But any history of bike thievery is conjecture.

Today is different. The civil wars occur more frequently and people take bikes. Lots and lots and lots of bikes. So many that most of the time people don't even bother filing reports (although there are a few efforts afoot to create regional registries). Still, if bike theft were a business, it would be a great investment. Here's how we'd size up a theoretical business:

- Strong revenue: check

- Low expenditures. Heavy-duty chisels and hammers cost between $20 and $30 at Home Depot. A 36-inch pair of bolt cutters is about the same. Check.

- Plant and development: none. Check.

- Recruiting: where there are college kids and the unemployed, you'll find your labor pool. Check.

- Workforce development. No recruiting or training costs. People train themselves and buy their own supplies. Check.

- Immunity to ups and downs in the economy. People steal things in good times and bad. Check.

- Compensation and benefits. You must be kidding. In the parlance of ancient Cro-Magnons and modern business-men, you eat what you kill.

- Risk: you could get caught, but it's highly unlikely. Snapping an insufficiently secured bike only takes a few seconds; and police have bigger crimes to solve than the case of the purloined Schwinns. Check.

- Room for growth: department stores and smaller retailers sell about 20 million bicycles annually, and sales are not limited to one part of the country. Check.

- Profitability: low costs, low risk, high revenue. Sounds like a good business model. Check.

Bike theft statistics won't overwhelm you. The FBI, the keeper of bike theft information, estimates that about 300,000 bikes are stolen annually, although it adds that only about one-third of all bike thefts are reported. For a country of 350 million people, that doesn't seem so bad (not that this is con-solation for anyone who was victimized). We've had bikes and individual parts stolen, and it always feels like a big violation of our space.

We live in larcenous times. In a story recounted on the com-pany website, in 1993 the founder of Kryptonite Locks locked a bicycle to a New York street pole to prove the greatness of his U-shaped creation. Within a week, all that remained was the lock. It's clearly a good tale for demonstrating the quality of his product—deservedly. Except for the period in the early 2000s when someone discovered that a plastic Bic pen could pick some of Kryptonite's round key locks and the company had to replace more than 400,000 locks with flat-key models, Kryptonite has had a good reputation. It's still the most common brand in bike shops, although you'll find excellent products from Master Lock and OnGuard.

Still, we were more struck by how a bike could literally disappear on a busy street in one of the world's busiest cities. Granted, New York is among the world's leaders in thieving hands. But we are sure that a similar experiment in many other cities would lend the same result.

Let us introduce you to Izzy Cortes. Izzy's been riding on city streets for most of his life. He says that he's been celebrating his 23rd birthday for 16 years. Over the past four years, he's made a good part of his living as a bike messenger in downtown Los Angeles. Now, we love L.A. It has the world's best taco stands this side of Guadalaraja, and you can ride in short sleeves in January while gazing at the snow-capped Angeles Mountain Range. It's also a good place to see movie stars. But for crime, let's put it this way. There are better places to park a bike.

Los Angeles bike messengers are street smart when it comes to urban cycling, and Izzy is savvy even by messenger standards. Yet in 2007, for about the first time in his adult life, Izzy took his eye off his bike for more than five seconds. It was gone. The story has a happy ending. Izzy saw the bike thief a few hours later and tracked him to an apartment building where police recovered the bike. Still, we figure if theft could happen to him, it could happen to anyone.

Of all the numbers related to bike theft, here is one that especially knocked us over. For much of the past decade, the

Dutch have averaged 700,000 stolen bikes per year. In the bike mecca of Amsterdam alone, 50,000 bikes were stolen. What does that mean?

It says that a country with decidedly pacifist tendencies, and the world's most passionate bike love affair—a people that have built multilevel bike garages and own 18 million bicycles—love to steal bikes, too.

You'll need a lock.

Maybe even two or three, say some experts.

Even then, your bike will not be impregnable.

We have learned that just as was the case with helmets, there are no guarantees. If a thief possesses the time and tools, he will find a way to cut through a lock. A bolt cutter will slice through a cable or a Master Lock in less time than it takes to butter your bread. U-locks, monster chains, padlocks, and combination locks all have their weak spots. Five years ago, the Slate.com writer Scott Elder wrote an amusing article on testing eight leading brands. He tried to disassemble eight different locks using a bike thief's common tools—crowbar, hammer, bolt cutter, and hacksaw with several blades. Elder rated each lock for security, portability, ease of use, and value to come up with a total. Each of the eight locks had weaknesses. Some were easy to break through. Others were heavy and difficult to carry. For unbreakability, there was a clear delineation between the four best and bottom performers. Elder scored the two monster chains, The OnGuard Beast and Kryptonite New York Chain, and two extra-thick U-locks, the OnGuard Brute and Kryptonite New York Fahgettaboutit, at roughly double the other locks in his survey.

The Fahgettaboutit, which ranked first, is distinctive by its yellow bar. Crafted of super-hardened steel, it is heavy but relatively compact. Elder could barely scratch the surface of the 18-millimeter shackle (the U) after five minutes of hack-sawing. Kryptonite certainly believes in the product, offering a $4,500 antitheft warranty. Elder didn't make much more progress sawing the Brute or in attacking the two superchains with bolt cutters, sawing, and hammering.

A monster chain with U-lock combo that is part of the Fahgettaboutit name received a thumbs-up in a more recent *Bicycling* magazine review. "No bike lock will protect from the most tenacious of thieves—locks are deterrents designed to make theft a pain in the neck—but the Faghettaboutit takes deterrence to a new level," the reviewer writes. The links are made of triple-heated boron manganese steel and are 11 millimeters thick. That's thick. But the chain is heavy at 20 pounds—try carting that over a business suit—and expensive at $130. Unless you're looking to secure multiple bikes in a terrible neighborhood, the U-lock Fahgettaboutit is a more reasonably priced alternative at $75–$90 online.

At the other end of the cost and ruggedness spectrum is the Master Pit Stop. The Pit Stop is for people who don't face serious security issues. This may sound unlikely in cities, but it is possible. The Pit Stop is certainly appropriate for a "what, me worry?" sort of client. The product's 2 feet of thin cable coils into a colored plastic case. The cases are about the size of a compact and available in primary colors or silver. The Pit Stop costs just $13. A U-lock of average density will cost two to three times that.

Yet what locks do effectively is create an obstacle, delaying the time it takes to steal your bike. Thieves like to go about their business quickly and painlessly. Izzy Cortes said that thieves typically scout a bike that looks enticing before pulling out tools to attack the lock in a rush. The more work involved—even a few extra seconds—the less likely they are to go after their bike. "Folks say, given enough time and tools, anything can be defeated," said Darryl Slater, a Kryptonite spokesperson. "Unless you've parked your bike in an abandoned alley, someone will say something if they see people working on a lock for a long time."

Every lock has advantages and disadvantages. We wanted to know what they were, so we spoke to the people who know best: messengers past and present, urban cyclists, bike shop owners, a Kryptonite representative, and a Los Angeles lock and key shop to the stars. We do not offer recommendations, but based on our thumbnail summaries, you'll be able to extrapolate which lock will suit you best.

Chains and monster chains: You can still create a chain the old-fashioned way by visiting a hardware store and having them unspool chain links. The thicker the links, the more difficult the chain will be to snap. But even the thickest chain usually carried by the average big-box or corner store won't measure up in effectiveness to the best Kryptonite or OnGuard chains. Chains (not monster chains) may be an effective, secondary option, snaked through wheels and seat posts and wrapped around thick poles that won't accommodate a U-lock.

Monster chains are a bit unwieldy for threading through frames, but they offer the same capacity for using voluminous street fixtures. They are a more effective alternative as a primary lock in high-crime, urban zones. They lose points because they're heavy and difficult to transport. You can't shove them into a messenger bag or small backpack unless it's the only thing you're carrying. Cortes' Kryptonite chain weighs 17 pounds. He wears it like a bandolier and uses it in combination with a U-lock. "I can wrap one around big poles and use the U-lock to secure one of the wheels," he said. One more note: chains can scratch bicycle paint. Some messengers wrap them in rubber sleeves, which may also help deter thieves.

U-lock: Kryptonite's signature product comes in different sizes. These are strong, easily portable locks. An 11" Kryptonite Evolution 4 LS, or similarly sized OnGuard U-lock will provide enough security for most situations. The shackle or U part of the Kryptonite lock and crossbar are crafted of 14-millimeter steel. Evolution series locks are recognizable by their orange crossbar. Kryptonite's top-line New York series locks—known for their yellow crossbars—are 16 or 18 millimeters thick. The company's New York minilock—just 3.25" wide by 6" long—offers a particular challenge because it offers so little surface space to attack. "Less usable space is more secure," said Darryl Slater. "It lets the thief get fewer tools in there, less leverage." For all their qualities, U-locks are limited in reach. The longest of Kryptonite's U-locks is just under a foot long. Because the shackle is inflexible, it cannot extend around thicker street fixtures.

Cable lock: Here's an example of what happens when you don't take time to do a little research and thinking. We tell the story so you won't make the same mistake. A bike shop

U-Locks are generally the best way to deter a bike thief.

mechanic once told us that a coiled cable lock was the best among locks. He said that the coils would foil bolt cutters. We purchased the lock at a time when Kryptonite U-locks were having trouble with Bic pens. The cable lock did save us a few dollars, but we have learned more about cable locks, namely that they won't foil bolt cutters anymore than a pack of gum. "Sure, they're easy to cut," said a locksmith at Los Feliz Lock & Key. Cable does have merits. It's flexible. It's easy to carry around. We recommend it as a secondary lock spun through your wheels or seat post, or if you're planning to move to Singapore, which lashes people for spitting gum on the street. We have not inquired about the country's punitive code for theft but assume that someone in Singapore would not dare steel a bicycle, lest they spend the rest of his or her life in chains.

Cost

You can find a good bike lock for between $20 and $40. OnGuard's Bulldog series of U-locks range in price from $15 to $25 online. The Bulldog series, the company's low-end line best suited for low to moderate crime areas, uses 11–13-millimeter shackles. Our 13-millimeter Kryptolok Series 2 lock cost $30 at a Los Angeles retailer. Darryl Slater said that the Kryptolok series is popular on college campuses, which traditionally have high rates of bike theft. Our lock has performed admirably in Los Angeles, although we never leave our bike in high-crime areas or out of sight for long periods. We occasionally also take our cable lock out of mothballs. A decade ago, it cost about $20. Top-of-the-line locks can be three times the cost of lower-end models. An OnGuard 7" Brute lock with a 17-millimeter steel shackle costs $65 on one website. The Kryptonite Fahgettaboutit 5" chain with 18-millimeter mini U-lock combo runs about $160. The Mini without the chain is about $55.

Transportability

U-lock manufacturers produce frame mounts. Like many products, most of them *ain't* what they used to be. They are made of plastic and prone to cracking. Our two cents on the matter: if you're very careful with them, perhaps you can make them last, oh, say, about two weeks. You might do better relying on your backpack, messenger bag, or pannier to hold them. The good news is that most locks will fit comfortably into any of the above. If you opt for a chain, the good news is that transporting it will require you to drape it over your body. The extra weight will have you burning more calories.

How Many Locks?

When we grew up, some hardware store–quality chain and a Master Lock was enough to thwart all but the most determined thieves. It may not even have been that they couldn't snap the chain. But rather, we liked to think that thieves had principles in the olden days. Chains meant something: off-limits, you've been outsmarted, try somewhere else. We're not saying there was any real logic to our boyhood thinking. We just can't remember too many times when a chained bicycle went missing. Of course, we grew up in nice communities, so maybe the criminals were soft.

Anyway, who would question that the criminal class has become more brazen? The run-of-the-mill lock is just an inconvenience now to be pulled apart with cutters, grinders, or some other devious device.

Most bike crooks carry their own bag of tools for solving locks. That's required the urban cyclist to counter. Urban cyclist Christopher Rommelmann said that some years ago it became common among his cycling buddies to carry two chains and that some of them are now using three—two U-locks and a big chain. Rommelmann is a good person to speak with about bike trends. He's a burly character straight out of Brooklyn, with the accent to match. He rode bike races in Central Park when he wasn't playing drums in a rock-and-roll band or working as a bike messenger in lower New York. In the early 1980s, he was one of the few bicyclists commuting over the Brooklyn Bridge. He road a fixie before people started using the term. Rommelmann also wore a beret—he had several. "People knew me for the hat," he said. "The cars and trucks weren't looking for you, and the bridge had these metal plates. I was always glad to see the Manhattan side."

Rommelmann himself uses two locks on the few occasions when he has to park his bicycle on the street out of eyesight. "It's safer that way," he said.

What's the Best Way to Lock up Your Bike?

We are generally of the belief that simple is best. We like basic black in our cycling clothes, grilled cheese sandwiches, and short goodbyes, not necessarily in that order. If you're working with a U-lock, we suggest the T-W-P method of security.

Tube-Wheel-Pole.

Slot the shackle—the U part of the lock—through the front tube (T).

Extend it though the wheel (W).

Nudge the U as far as it will go around a convenient pole (P). Then lock the bar end closed—more on key care in a moment.

We will assume that you need little direction with the unlocking and locking part of the operation. However, we would add that in the unlikely event that a key jams, perhaps after a would-be intruder has maliciously done something, Do Not Force It! We have found through the years that no good things happen

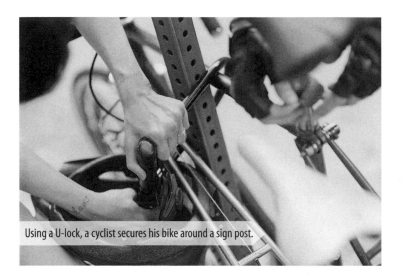

Using a U-lock, a cyclist secures his bike around a sign post.

in trying to force a key, and we refer to separate weekend visits by locksmiths to our car and home.

Another note: avoid the lazy person's approach of dragging your bicycle by the lock. It's a good way to damage a spoke or ding your frame. If you're not close enough to where you'll be securing the bike, pick it up. Better yet, position your bicycle first and then lock.

Now we come to a favorite topic: key care. At least one of us considers himself one of the world's leading experts on the subject because of the sheer volume of keys he has lost through the years. These include home, bike, locker, filing cabinet, and antique chests. We also have a container of keys for which we cannot find locks.

That is why we urge you upon purchasing your lock to immediately separate your keys. Lock manufacturers provide two, sometimes three (Kryptonite produces a lighted key for nighttime locking). Keep your reserve key or keys in a place that's safe and easy to remember.

Kryptonite, OnGuard, and Master Lock provide a service where you can register your lock number. If you lose both keys, the companies will send you reserves for a small fee. Regarding the primary key, we urge you to put it on your key chain instead of keeping it separately. You're almost always going to have your key chain on you, which makes it unlikely you'll bring your bike lock but not the key.

Securing Other Parts of Your Bike

You know how it is in cities. If something isn't tied down, it's gone when you return. That includes bicycles, for which there is a lively trade in secondhand parts. Double-lock an unremarkable REI hybrid to a lamppost. If it has a top-grade saddle, the bike may survive but not the seat.

"If you have a nice saddle, a Brooks or competition saddle, some thief will want it," said Izzy Cortes.

Brooks leather saddles can cost as much as $300 online based on a recent search. That's about the price of an inexpensive hybrid bike. Cortes uses a Brooks on one of the two bikes he alternates for work and commuting to his second job in a Melrose Boulevard bike shop. He mounts a two-level defense. First, he stuffs the locking mechanism that secures the seat post to the frame with superglue and ball bearings. "Inside where the Allen key goes," said Cortes. Some people use wax.

Cortes isn't growing, so won't need to adjust the seat, and that if he does want to change the height, he can use solvent to dissolve the glue. Then he loops a chain housed in a rubber sleeve through the seat stays that connect the saddle to the seat post. You can use a thinner cable to accomplish the same task, too. "Even if someone makes it through the ball bearings, they can't take the saddle off," Cortes said.

How the Police Lock Up Their Bikes

Both the bike thefts that one author experienced over the years occurred under similar circumstances even though one was in Chicago and one was in a small town in Virginia—both happened in a shaded, out-of-the-way area with little foot traffic, perfect for a thief.

"Park in front of a busy business," suggested Bill Jackson, a 10-year cycling commuter in Chicago. "Use lots of locks and make sure to lock both wheel and seat post if you can. I use a cable, a U-lock and a cable lock when I lock my bike. I do remove the front wheel and use a cable, too, if I can, but if you haven't had someone at a shop show you how to remove and reinstall the wheel, you're better off locking it all up in place."

We talked with a couple of bicycle police officers about how they lock their bikes.

Use a cable and U-lock. Wind the cable through your front wheel and then take one looped end of the cable and feed it through the opposite end to form a garrote that cinches your front wheel to the bike frame.

Now take the free end of the cable and let it dangle to the ground while you slide your U-lock through the rear wheel. You want to slide the U-lock through the rear of the bike so that the bike rack you are locking up to is inside the U-lock's two extensions.

Be sure that both the rear wheel and part of the bike frame are within the U-lock.

Now simply loop the end of your cable that's free over one of the extenders and close the U-lock in place.

You should now have your rear wheel firmly locked to the post and

A heavy-duty chain and U-lock combination is usually the most difficult lock to break through.

Registries and Social Media

The National Bike Registry charges $10 for a 10-year registration or $25 for 30 years. You can also purchase a family plan, up to five bikes registered for 10 years each. The registration entitles you to a "tamperproof" decal. This assumes that police or someone else will not only see the decal, but realize on the spot that the bike is stolen. It also assumes, at least for the longer plan, that you will be holding on to your bike for 30 years. It may not be the best option if you're already 55. Stolen bike registry sends stolen bike listings from Tucson, Chicago, San Francisco, Berkley, San Diego, Seattle, and Philadelphia to Twitter accounts listing stolen bikes in those cities. On a more informal level, we have also heard of people recovering

the cable threaded through your front wheel with one end of the cable also locked to the post.

Some cyclists will carry two U-locks and simply lock up both wheels to a solid object, which is a more secure way to lock your bike. However, carrying two heavy U-locks can grow tiresome quickly.

But your security isn't complete yet.

Remove your bike's computer, bottle, lights, and any other additions that can be simply taken by passersby. We have had cheap horns and even stickers stolen from bikes, which, apparently (and unfortunately), isn't all that uncommon.

"This is the most important though," Jackson added. "Whenever you leave your bike anywhere, even if you've only been in the store for 15 minutes, check all the quick releases. I've had people loosen them. Why? Beats me, but I know when they come undone, it can be really, really ugly."

How ugly? Imagine mounting your bike only to find that somebody loosened your front wheel. It won't take you long to realize something is wrong. By then you just might be in the middle of an intersection when your wheel comes off and learn that there are worse things a person can do to your bike than steal it.

stolen bikes via postings on their Facebook page. We support any effort to make it easier for people to recover stolen property of any sort, but we're also realists. Once you've had a bike stolen, its unlikely you'll find it unless you attach a location signal similar to the one used by the bad guys in *No Country for Old Men*.

Final Notes

One of us once allowed someone to borrow a bike. It was many years ago in front of a red schoolhouse in Queens. The bike was new, a purple Schwinn Sting-Ray on one of its first rides. The borrower seemed nice enough. He was a regular at the playground, in his early teens. He took a turn around the yard, then another, and another, a little faster with each lap. Then he disappeared with the bike. We never saw it again. Fifteen years later, living in a different, less crime-ridden city, we left a bike unattended, and we hesitate to admit unlocked, while we returned to our apartment building's lobby to fetch our mail. The bike was out of sight for less than two minutes. We never saw it again. The lesson of the stories: cities are tough places. Never feel too secure. Never leave an unlocked bike unattended. Never try to save money on locks. Kryptonite's Darryl Slater said you should spend about 10 percent of the cost of your bike on locks. Make your mantra "better safe than sorry." And never trust anyone with your purple Sting-Ray.

8

Safety Cycling

How to Survive by Being Bold
and Following the Rules of the Road

Perhaps the biggest obstacle to becoming an urban cyclist is the thought of riding amidst traffic. We do not mean simply the sheer number of cars that you will encounter but rather the potent combination of volume and unpredictability. You will not be able to anticipate what many cars will do. Those include the seemingly safest, most law-abiding drivers. Good intentions do not preclude the occasional careless act.

In another chapter, we describe accidents that we and other urban cyclists have suffered—unexpected decelerations, car door openings, and sudden turns. We've done this not so much to discourage you but as to ready you for the volatility you may face.

Forewarned is forearmed. Or is it the reverse?

Otherwise, cyclists can exert considerable control over their fates by heeding common sense and following the same rules as drivers. To those of you who don't drive, common sense and rules of the road are almost the same. You slow down and stop when you're supposed to slow down and stop, signal for turns, and watch out for what the other guy or gal is doing. It also helps to drive straight unless you're avoiding big objects. The Dutch require their children to take a course in cycling safety. That befits a country that averages more than a bicycle per person. The U.S. has no national program. That befits a country where cycling participation still hasn't had a breakthrough.

There are excellent resources. For a quick fix, we point you to the League of American Bicyclists website (www.bikeleague.org), which covers nine Rules of the Road. The rules include tips for lane positioning and changing, turning, and how far you should ride to the right. We like John Allen's *Bicycling Street Smarts*, a 46-page guidebook on "Riding Confidently, Legally, and Safely." It is among the country's most widely circulated texts on cycling, and with good reason. It is short, well written, and encompasses a great deal of material. An engineer by training, Allen became a cycling advocate.

We would also mention John Forester's nearly 600-page opus, *Effective Cycling*, perhaps the single most comprehensive, consumer-oriented U.S. cycling book. Over the past three decades, Forester has been one of the giants in noncompetitive U.S. cycling, a former president of the League of American Wheelmen, the roughly century-old organization that became the League of American Cyclists, and advocate for cyclists' rights.

Forester's overriding and somewhat controversial message at a time when cyclists on the street were much rarer than today was that they had the same entitlement to the road as drivers. It is more accepted today than it was more than three decades ago when Forrester became interested in cycling, although we stop short of saying that everyone accepts his idea.

Many people in our car-crazy culture believe that cyclists must always defer to drivers—and quickly—or that they really belong on sidewalks. The sidewalk is, with the exception of children and rare circumstances, exactly where cyclists should not be. The cyclist doubter equates the megahorsepower of the car with hegemony. But one has nothing to do with the other. Although a few states have individual laws that favor cars, the cyclist is the equal of the driver.

With such status comes responsibility for cyclists. It means obeying the rules of the road. It means riding in a manner that does not put you or others in danger. We won't list everything you can do here. Rather, we'll tackle some of the most important dos and don'ts.

Don't Be a Weaver

Don't you hate it when someone behaves erratically? You don't know how to respond. You wind up frustrated and short-tempered. Drivers feel the same way when they have to deal with a cyclist who's weaving all over the road. Do they dare pass, even when the rules of the road permit, or hold steady at an unfairly slow pace, waiting for the discourteous cyclist to head definitively in one direction? We'll speak more about cycling courtesy and civility shortly. Suffice it to say that you should cycle predictably. Hold a steady line and make firm decisions so that drivers and others can respond in kind.

Or a Threader

It's particularly tempting to thread through traffic that's stopped or inching along. As a cyclist, your narrow berth and mobility allows you to squeeze through the lineup of cars. Don't do it.

Even wide bike lines don't have a lot of room. Drive straight.

We're not saying that you should never change lanes or stop searching for safe pockets of free space. Rather, we're saying that you shouldn't be riding on lane markers or other boundaries, or move from lane to lane whenever the mood strikes. That's a quick way to an accident. We invite you to think risk-reward when you're cycling. Is the risk of doing something worth the payoff? With threading, it's not.

Follow Traffic Signs and Signals

Signs and signal lights are a big part of ensuring that streets don't deteriorate into anarchy. As a cyclist, you're no less obligated to obey them than a driver. By doing so, you navigate potential dangers and contribute to a system that gives everyone a better chance of predicting each other's moves. We know that there will be moments, late at night, on deserted streets, when you'll be tempted to ignore road governance. We encourage you to think deeply before acting.

Cyclists must obey the same traffic rules as drivers, including halting at stop signs.

Don't Ride Facing Traffic

Some people think that it's safer to ride against traffic than with it. They say that you'll be able to better see potential danger sooner and scoot out of the way. We remind you again of the importance of being predictable when you cycle. If drivers know what you're going to do, they can respond safely. If they don't, the likelihood of an accident increases. Drivers and others don't usually expect cyclists to be riding against traffic. So they may turn without looking. Ride with traffic. People expect it.

Don't Ride Too Far Right

It will be temping to ride as far right as possible. You may believe that nothing can happen when you're near the curb or shoulder, far away from traffic. Yet lots can happen. There's usually more debris and rough spots to upset your balance. Riding too far right will also make it difficult for drivers to see you. A car's biggest blind spot is usually to the right and rear. Some meaner drivers may also try to pinch you farther right. Don't give an inch so cars can take a yard. Cycle in regular traffic lanes whenever possible. The law entitles you to as much.

Scan for Obstacles

It would be nice if all you had to do as a cyclist was look straight ahead. But danger sometimes lurks on the ground. An old boot, a sharp can, and other objects can trip you up or force you to swerve suddenly at your own risk. We recommend looking ahead on the ground, not just at eye level.

Stop When You Need to and Find a Safe Haven

We hope that you'll never feel threatened or boxed in. But we know that there are drivers with questionable notions of caution, and city streets often don't leave you much room to maneuver. No one's forcing you to drive on. If you feel endangered, sometimes it's best to pull off the road at the first safe place.

Don't Be Cowed by Impatient Drivers

Let's assume that you're riding in a lane the way that you're supposed to and that a driver lets you know via his car's proximity to your back wheel, use of the horn, or harsh language that he wants you to move over. If there's a place to pull to the side, be courteous, by all means. But if there's nowhere to go, or you're about to turn, you have no obligation to move. You belong on the road as much as the car. In these situations, consider yourself a defender of urban cyclists everywhere.

Sidewalks Are Not for Bikes

Nearly all laws in the United States regarding bicycles are handled at the state level. That means that laws will vary slightly from state to state and that includes riding on a sidewalk. Most states make it illegal to bicycle on a sidewalk if the cyclist is over the age of 12.

If the right edge of a street is in such poor shape that you cannot safely ride on it, then you are expected to ride in the car lane, not the sidewalk. Given the option between riding down the center of a busy traffic lane or riding on the sidewalk, many cyclists choose the sidewalk. However, you must understand that it is not advised. If you collide with a pedestrian, you are most likely going to be found at fault.

No matter if it's legal or illegal, bicycling on a sidewalk is an easy way to get in trouble. Pedestrians hate dodging bicycles going faster than they on a stretch built for foot traffic. Die-hard cyclists hate those who ride on sidewalks because it gives cyclists a bad name and leads to aggression between cyclists and pedestrians. It's a horrible idea and can quickly lead to altercations and problems even if you are a toddler.

In October 2010, a lawyer in New York City sued two 4-year-old children who were riding their bicycles on a Manhattan sidewalk and hit the lawyer's 87-year-old mother, who broke her hip and died two months later.

But Be Courteous

Courteous cyclists share the road. They signal clearly and well in advance, so that drivers know what they're going to do. When it's safe, they pull to the side to allow cars to pass. They are not combative, even when they are in the right. They do not slap the rear panels of cars that seem to have behaved improperly or engage in shouting matches with rude drivers. They remain calm, and in this way they do credit to cyclists everywhere.

Don't Treat Bike Lanes as Security Blankets

Bike lanes are not automatic safe havens. While we believe that bike lanes force drivers to pay a little closer attention, they cannot guarantee that drivers will stay in their own lane or look for cyclists on every turn. If we're starting to sound like nervous parents who repeat everything a dozen times just in case their kids haven't heard their warnings, so be it. We'll say what we've said in other instances: proceed with caution. We say the same even with bike lanes separated from car traffic. You may not have to worry about drivers, but careless cyclists can also do you harm if you're not alert.

Slow Up if a Bus or Truck Speeds Up as You're Trying to Pass

Buses and garbage trucks stop frequently. Many of them sport bumper stickers saying as much. But sometimes they stop for a shorter period of time than you expect. If that happens while you're trying to pass, don't force things. Even if you're in the right, or think that you can clear the front bumper, which is what driver's education instructors teach you about passing safely, the reward doesn't justify the risk. Buses and trucks may be slow out of the gate, but once they get rolling, they're faster than you.

Make Sure the Driver Can See You

As you approach an intersection going one way, you may think that a car stopped at a stop sign or signal light is unlikely to advance. You may think the same in other situations, and most of the time, you will be right. But what if you're wrong—even just once? You can take a more proactive stance by slowing a little and making eye contact with the driver. The extra effort is a way to ensure that he or she has seen you and that you are

Clear signaling is important for any cyclist.

right in assuming that the car won't be jetting into your path. In cycling or driving, anything that enhances communication makes things safer.

Don't Pass on the Right, Particularly if It's a Bus or Van

One of the first rules in driving is not to pass on the right. Faster traffic is supposed to stay to the left, where it's easier for other drivers to see cars. The same wisdom holds for cycling, and then some. Drivers don't look as much for vehicles to pass them on the right. Add that cyclists are smaller and more difficult to see in rearview mirrors or via quick glances. Even if it feels awkward pulling farther into the street, it's safer because you'll be easier to spot. That includes passing slower traffic.

Being Predictable Will Save Your Life (And Aggressiveness Is Your Ally)

It may go against your natural instincts, but working to be the first wheels through a busy intersection will likely save you from injury.

A cyclist is the most vulnerable when going from a full stop to starting to pedal. It takes hundreds of miles of practice to reduce or avoid the natural side-to-side swing in handlebars that occurs when most cyclists begin riding. Many experienced cyclists will strive to avoid coming to a complete stop for the purposes of maintaining their forward progress and working to establish their position at the crosswalk for when the light changes and bikes and cars have to converge.

Aggressiveness is your friend in this situation, and going hand-in-hand with that aggressiveness is the need to get your bike to 10 mph as quickly as possible. There are two main reasons for this:

1) Being the first through any intersection gives you the immediate advantage of establishing your presence in the bike lane on the other side of the intersection. It allows the drivers behind you to see where you are and predict where you are going.

2) A bike is at its most uncontrollable at the slowest speeds. Experience indicates that it is not until roughly 10 mph that the average cyclist will cease swaying back and forth in traffic and be able to maintain a solid, upright, and predictable pathway.

But it isn't as simple as "being first" through an intersection. It's just as important that your actions are predictable to those around you. Erratically making a left-hand turn from the far-right lane is not only illegal, but a good way to start an accident if you are a motorist. However, the same action by a cyclist could get the rider killed.

"Ride predictably," cautioned Bill Jackson, who has commuted to work on his bike for 10 years in Chicago. "If you're weaving around, you're freaking out your fellow riders and folks in cars. If a car doesn't know if you're going to stop for a light or a sign, it makes it harder on them to know where to be so they don't hit you."

Aggressiveness in this instance is *not* about being first or any foolish notions of braggadocio. It is simply acknowledging that two vastly different vehicles—large, heavy cars and small, light bicycles—must occupy tight quarters while moving forward at increasing speeds. If you are the first to occupy that territory (in this case, we're focusing on the

Communicate with drivers, particularly at busy intersections.

start of the bike lane on the far side of the intersection), then drivers know where you are going to be and can drive accordingly, meaning they can swerve around you.

If you allow drivers to be the first through intersections, you have to follow their lead and hope that they leave you enough room. Considering that most motorists have so many other things to think about—driving the speed limit, watching for police, and paying attention to lights and signs, not to mention distractions like singing to a song, texting, and/ or talking on the phone or just thinking about their day—it is naïve to think that a motorist will have your well-being in mind.

This is not an attack on motorists; it is simply acknowledging the reality in today's urban setting.

None of this has to be confrontational. In fact, experienced riders will tell you quickly that having an adversarial attitude toward other vehicles is not conducive to a pleasant ride, much less a healthy one.

"A look with an added smile or friendly wave produces such a great environment for everyone that I was amazed how positive the results were when I started riding in a better mood," said Bryan Finigan, a former bike messenger and bike mechanic who has commuted on city streets for more than 20 years. "I have followed this school of thought for two years now and can say it has profoundly affected my ride."

Don't Force Things at Intersections

Intersections aren't opportunities to play chicken or demonstrate newfound speed as lights are about to turn. Green is for go, but contrary to the old joke, yellow doesn't mean go faster. Driving guidelines teach proceeding with caution on yellow. The same guidelines apply for cycling on yellow and at any busy intersection. The cautious approach will give you extra time to anticipate potential dangers and react.

Ride to the Center of the Right Lane for Right Turns

It may seem safer to squeeze as far right as possible when you want to make a right turn. But as we've mentioned previously, squeezing right reduces your visibility to drivers. If one of those drivers decides to turn right, you may be pinched dangerously close to a curb.

Ride to the Left to Make a Left Turn

You'll have to be a little brave the first couple of times you make a left turn. We say *a little* because wading farther into traffic is exactly what doesn't feel safe. A bicycle would seem to be an easy target in the middle of a busy street. But if you ride safely and with confidence, you won't have a problem. If you're in the right lane, start looking for a safe opening as far in advance as possible to move to the left. If you're turning from the left lane of a four-lane road, position yourself in the middle of the lane. That way, drivers will be able to see you easily and won't be able to pass on the right side. (You always want to keep cars and faster cyclists to your left.) The same goes for turning from a turn lane. In both cases, once you clear the intersection, you'll move quickly to the right, allowing cars behind you to pass safely. This is good cycling etiquette.

It's Not a Race

Your ride is *not* a race. It may feel like one—maybe a time trial to beat your personal-best commute—but treating it as such is dangerous to yourself and others.

"I couldn't agree with this more," said Bill Jackson, who has competed in cyclocross races since 2005 and has been a daily cycling commuter since 2001. "My races are on Sunday. So, if it's not Sunday, there's no reason to race. That's my mantra I tell myself over and over again. Also, I never ride with a stopwatch or timer. I figure I'll get there when I get there. It makes for less stress and means I'm less likely to be agitated and sweaty when I get where I am [going]. I also leave as much time as I can so I don't have to hurry. I've seen wrecks where folks just are trying to make up too much time."

When I first began bike commuting, I was eager to improve my numbers—highest speed, fastest one-way commute, fewest stop lights encountered, etc. Anyone who has grown up playing sports and working out has a basic approach generally drilled into him or her by coaches and trainers—improve your numbers, whether that's lowering your 40-yard dash time or increasing your bench press weight and reps.

But that thinking can get you killed when cycling.

I used to commute to work on Chicago's bike path and would ride casually until someone passed me. As soon as that happened, I changed. Like my dog going from stoic pose to attack after seeing a squirrel in a tree, I would change my ride from a simple commute to a race against some stranger who didn't know we were "racing." After several near accidents, I realized that I was needlessly putting at risk my health and the health of others.

There is no race.

Nobody is timing you.

You are the only one concerned with your ride.

Enjoy yourself. You'll have plenty to worry about when you get to work, home, or other destinations.

—S.R.

Go to the Middle of the Right Lane When Going Through an Intersection

If you intend to ride straight, it's important to move to the center of the right lane before entering the intersection. This will prevent right-turning cars from cutting you off, or worse, plowing into you as you hug the right. Ride swiftly through the intersection and then move to the right to allow faster traffic to pass.

Beware Tracks, Raised Lane Dots, and Grates

Tracks are for trains. Lane dots are for drivers. Grates are for sewer rats. None were created with cyclists in mind. In some cases, they may become booby traps, jolting you off balance, or in the case of grates, trapping your front wheel. You must

B.U.I.—Bicycling Under the Influence

While most states have laws that say operating a bicycle under the influence of drugs or alcohol is illegal, the standards for deciding such an infraction vary.

There are varying levels of what is considered legally intoxicated based on your blood alcohol content, but that's not the real sticking issue. The most complicated element is defining a vehicle.

For example, Oregon and California consider a bicycle to be the same as a car, so you can be charged with a BUI for bicycling home from the local pub just as if you were driving your car drunk. However, states like South Dakota and New York do not consider bicycles as vehicles. You can be arrested for public drunkenness, but will not be charged with operating a vehicle.

In many states, the definition of vehicle hinges on whether a motor is involved. If human or animal power is used, it is not a vehicle. According to *New York Times* journalist David Goodman, bicyclists have a horse to thank for the two standards: "The landmark case in local B.U.I. law, such as it is, did not actually involve a bicycle. In 1970, the police arrested Bernard Szymanski for piloting a horse-drawn carriage while drunk. A be especially wary of all of these when streets are wet. Ride more cautiously when you approach any of them. The wet manhole is also treacherous. When metal becomes slick, it's easy to lose traction. Go easy and find another place to turn.

Brake Gradually Into Downhill Curves

It's easy to get carried away on downhills. They can feel like amusement park rides. Beware the temptation to lose all sense of caution, though. The faster you go, the shorter your reaction time. That can be troublesome if a car unexpectedly turns into your lane. Driving moderately downhill is especially good policy if there's) a curve at the bottom. Curves prevent you from seeing beyond them. When you can't see what's ahead, the risk of an accident increases.

judge dismissed the case, noting, with some chagrin, that the statutes applied only to 'motor vehicles,' and not those under horse—or human—power, like bicycles."

Goodman's article followed a growing and alarmingly bad idea in U.S. cities—bicycle crawls. A pub crawl is a party that moves from bar to bar with partiers having a drink or two at each stop. A bicycle crawl is the same, except that bikes are used, allowing partiers to pick bars that are farther apart.

We're all for good times, but we know how badly you can hurt yourself when trying to operate a bicycle while high or drunk.

Consider the right forearm of one of the authors for proof. During a college party, this author tried a friend's bike and wasn't used to the braking system, which led to him running into a curb at full speed. The bike stopped instantly, but the author went flying with his arms extended in front of him as if he was still holding on to the handlebars. He slid down the sidewalk like he was diving head first into home plate. The road rash went from elbow to wrist and 20 years later the scars are still there. Thankfully, this accident happened in an empty parking lot, not on a city street where a vehicle could have run him over.

If you want to drink, take a cab.

Don't Play Follow the Leader

Sometimes you fall into the same rhythm as a cyclist in front of you. The distance between you is constant. You're lulled into a sense of security. But don't emulate the other rider's every move. He or she may not be making sound riding decisions. The cyclist you're following may also face different factors than you will. It only takes a couple of seconds for a car that was not a problem for one cyclist at an intersection to be very much so for a second cyclist.

Report Drivers Who Purposely Endanger You

If someone approached you in a restaurant, pulled out a crowbar, and took a swing at your head, you'd call the police (after doing your best Usain Bolt imitation to a safe place). Consider a driver with bad intentions a bigger, more dangerous version of the crowbar swinger. At least with a crowbar, you're on your feet and not as vulnerable as you are on a bike encountering someone wielding a two-tons-plus weapon. And make no mistake: cars used to hurt people are weapons. If someone hits you, or even if he or she doesn't hit you but clearly wants to, remember the license plate and car type and report it to the police. You may be able to file charges.

Jump Over Deep Potholes

Riding through a deep pothole is a treacherous experience. If the hole is large enough, you may go flying, or at least have to steady your balance. Remember how you used to jump curbs and small obstacles by pulling up on the handlebars? It's the same thing here to leap the hole. Summon your inner child. Have fun.

9

Packing Gear and Techniques

You're Not Handicapped Just Because
You Don't Have a Car Trunk

How much stuff do you cart around?

We're not speaking about those instances when you're helping your girlfriend or boyfriend move across town. You'll rent
a van then, or maybe two vans if there are lots of plants and a
stationary cycle. We're not speaking about those times when
you're switching jobs and carting a cardboard box of work
folders and mementos home or returning from the Costco run.

How often do you really fill the Volkswagen Jetta to the
gills, or even use the trunk?

Most of the time, your car is probably empty, save some
combination of your smartphone, laptop, a cup of Starbucks,

your workout clothes in a small nylon bag, and/or some groceries. We carry light these days. There's no regular lugging of files. Most of what we need we carry in electronic databases, accessible via a jab or two of our fingertips. The other resources appear where we need them—at work, school, the gym, or hotels. Even when we travel, we're packing everything into a case that squeezes into the equivalent of a large desk drawer.

Clearly, when we're going somewhere, we don't need much stuff.

The good news, amidst assorted other good news for cyclists, is that with interest in cycling as transportation growing, an increasing number of companies are producing items to make carting your belongings easier. "We're selling more of these baskets and accessories than anything else," said Julie Hirschfeld, the founder and owner of New York's Adeline Adeline bicycle shop.

Indeed, we can think of at least a half-dozen companies that manufacture quality panniers, rear racks, front and rear baskets, and trailers for little people or bigger things that won't fit on your bike. The trailers can even hold plants, provided they're not along the lines of a 10' royal palm tree. Many of the options are sturdy and waterproof, and with proper care will last as long as your bike. We'll address them front to rear.

Panniers

We love the word *pannier*. It sounds like a French pastry you should have with a café au lait on the Champs d'Elyssee. The word is an English adaptation of the old French word *panier*, meaning bread basket. For you Latin scholars, that word derives from the Latin words *panarium*, meaning basket for bread, and *panis*, which means bread and is similar to the modern French (*pain*) and Italian (*pane*) words for the same. We are

Panniers can hold 30 pounds of dog food.

particularly fond of the full definition of pannier: a basket, especially one of a pair slung over a beast of burden.

By literal definitions, the beast would be your bike, or what nineteenth-century inventors and thinkers dubbed the mechanical horse. But we have yet to find a bicycle that rides itself—electric bicycles still require someone to guide them.

You are the beast.

Panniers hang snugly over either side of the rear wheel, usually via hooking, Velcro, or slotting mechanisms that attach to the rear rack. If you plan to use your bicycle for transporting anything more than flowers, your French Bulldog, and some odds and ends, you will need a rear rack.

Some panniers—along with the racks—require tools to install. Some do not. Regardless, you will align the panniers in a logical manner, so that the pannier is stable, does not interfere with the rear wheel or chain, and is suitably distanced from your legs and the ground. For logical reasons, you should not be bumping into your panniers, and they should not be dragging like cow's utters.

To Pannier or Not Pannier

For many of us, backpacks have been part of our daily life since elementary school. So I never thought about trying panniers when I began commuting daily in 2004. I packed my backpack and took to the streets.

After thousands of miles, I began to notice my shoulders and back feeling the strain of the backpack, and it also made my back sweat more than was necessary. I found an Ortlieb waterproof pannier on sale for $60, bought it, and have been grateful ever since. I cannot imagine commuting without panniers now. The lack of extra weight pulling on my shoulders made my ride more enjoyable than it had been for years.

I felt like a fool for not making the switch sooner. I would urge any cyclist to get a pannier so long as they can get a waterproof one.

"Panniers are brilliant, urban or otherwise, to avoid the crippling effect of riding in a backpack, not to mention the issue of a sweaty back," said Julian Sayarer, who in December 2009 set the world record for fastest circumnavigation of the world on bicycle, finishing his 18,050-mile trek in 165 days. "No amount of bridge in the structure of a bag can compete with a simple pannier. Waterproof is obviously the No. 1 issue. For not much more in cost you can get a waterproof [pannier], so I can't see much point in buying non-waterproof versions."

Some experts believe that Ortlieb makes the best panniers, which is why the company's panniers are so popular. But in the interest of fairness to all manufacturers, we urge you to look at all pannier manufacturers and compare them before making your decision. Axiom is another

Panniers come in various colors and sizes.

Panniers come in different sizes. We recently read of a pair with a combined 110-liter capacity. We doubt you will ever need anything close to that volume, unless, of course, you are responsible for refreshments at the next Pittsburgh Steelers tailgate party. Most of the panniers we've seen in retail stores are of a far more reasonable size, but more than sufficient for carrying common urban supplies. A pair of Ortlieb panniers we recently found advertised for $165 at REI.com has a combined 2,441 cubic inches of space. That's enough to carry laptops and lunch for you and several cubicle mates.

Germany-based Ortlieb is among the leading manufacturers of panniers and is highly regarded for its sturdy constructions,

popular manufacturer with commuters as well as Action, Avenir, M-Wave, Schwinn, Seattle Sports, SunLite, and Topeak.

We would urge anyone purchasing a pannier to inspect it in person before buying. We also would urge that you go with a waterproof version even if you live in an arid location because rain and puddles are not the only liquids than can spill onto your pannier and potentially soak whatever is inside.

And be careful what you put in your pannier, warns one experienced cyclist.

"I would never place my laptop computer in a pannier or anywhere on the bicycle; that will always be on my person in a messenger bag," said Bryan Finigan, who has commuted and worked on bikes for more than 20 years in the Midwest. "I found a lot of value in [panniers] however it did take a bit of time to adjust to having the extra weight on the bike. I had to get used to the extra stopping distance required as well as just getting used to how the balance and the steering was affected. I believe that panniers for the bike commuters to hold extra clothing and lunch or for stopping at the grocery store have great value because most can easily be removed and reinstalled for when you wish."

—S.R

which include thick, waterproof materials and reinforced bottoms and sides. The company produces about 30 different panniers of different shapes and sizes, including those with hard shells and bags that can be worn messenger-bag style when they're detached. If you regularly buy out the local stop-and-shop, the company also sells so-called front rollers, panniers that fit over your front wheel and can match your rear panniers.

Other well-regarded pannier manufacturers are the British company Carradice, Jandd, Axiom Gear, Bruce Gordon, Radical Design, Rivendell, Two Wheel Gear, Vaude and Arkel, Linus, and Electra. REI also has its own small line of panniers. Gilles Berthould produces super-fancy panniers. Materials range from heavy-duty waterproof synthetics to natural fibers. Carradice produces a nifty line of canvas panniers and other bags that seem straight from a 1930s Egyptian bike trip. Linus sells a market bag with an extra layer of canvas to better absorb the moisture from all the fresh vegetables you'll be buying. San Diego-based Electra, which is better known for its European-style, internally hubbed bicycles, produces wicker saddlebags, which we saw for $100 online—very pastoral.

Other Bags

If you don't need panniers, there are bags that hook to other parts of the frame. New York shop Adeline Adeline sells Brooks leather tool bags that fit under the saddle and cost $110, a hefty sum for a bag that couldn't hold much more than two eyeglass cases. But it's Brooks, the famed manufacturer of high-quality, leather bicycle saddles, so the construction is top grade. The English company has been around almost as long as bicycles have. Adeline Adeline sells Pashley handlebar bags and a Retrovelo frame bag that fits over the top tube. It also has a canvas and leather front-mounted bag that looks straight out of the pages of *Vogue*. They'll all set you back at least $200, but add to your classiness quotient.

Our favorite picture on the Carradice company website shows a distinguished-looking, undoubtedly British gentleman, clad in a V-neck sweater and collar shirt, standing proudly next to a fold-up bike. Attached to the bike, perched between the handlebars and the front wheel, is a City Folder, a square canvas bag that seems ideal for carrying the morning paper, an iPad, or laptop in style.

Baskets

Baskets, along with bells, are the most iconic bicycle accessories. They speak to earlier times of boyhood paper routes and shopping in open markets. The latter activity has continued to thrive in Europe. Some accounts of bicycle history credit an African American inventor, JM Certain, for inventing the first basket. Drawings of Certain's parcel carrier, for which he received a patent on December 26, 1899, show two vaguely cone-like baskets bracketing a front wheel. In the ensuing

This bicycle features roomy front and rear baskets.

A wicker basket.

decades, baskets became a regular feature of bicycles. A number of companies manufactured them, but baskets were also of the home-scrabbled variety: wire, wicker, fruit baskets and boxes, or anything else that seemed durable enough and could be attached easily.

The current selection of baskets is wide. Shapes include oval to square to straight rectangle, to rectangle with rounded ends. Some baskets are flatter and longer. In our quick survey of baskets, we found that these tend to be of the steel-wire variety. Others are deep, hanging almost the entire length of the bike stem.

A few baskets have covers with or without fasteners. We liked a wicker number we saw at Adeline Adeline, an Abici square basket with a front rack for mounting and hinged top. The $130 price was not for the budget cyclist.

A few companies also make baskets specifically for smaller, four-legged companions. Basil's Pluto model combines a wicker bottom and steel-wire top, the latter to prevent Fido from introducing himself to the odd stray cat. Holland-based Basil lists nearly 200 types of baskets on its website.

Not all baskets sit in front. Julie Hirschfeld uses a Basil basket fitted to her bike's rear rack when she commutes from Brooklyn to New York. But most baskets hang or sit in front of the stem. They usually won't hold as much as panniers or sizable rear containers, but they are more easily accessible. However, we would advise you to double-check the fastenings, lest you ride off with your basket bobbing up and down like a buoy.

Most baskets are still made from metal or wicker, although a number of companies have introduced synthetics in recent years. Some of these resemble natural materials. They tend not to weather as gracefully but may last longer and are often environmentally friendly. The British retailer Hen & Hammock advertises a basket made from multicolored, used packaging tape. Basil manufactures a Blossom line of baskets from woven recycled materials. The Blossoms range in price from about $30 to $65 online. We admit to having a weak spot for Basil's milk carton baskets, also of several different hues. They remind us of the days that we used similar cartons to build four-wheeled mini-racers, our homemade mechanical horses. At the same time, we think you could craft your own milk carton basket with some strategically placed plastic ties or Velcro straps.

Basil also produces classic metal wire, wicker, and rattan baskets, as well as newer-wave steel mesh ones that can run more than $100. In our survey, we didn't see a basket costing more than $175. The least expensive were two relatively small models, one of wicker and the other of woven wood, that would handle a picnic lunch for two and not much more. Steel mesh is stronger than wicker, looks good in a modernist sort

A retro wire and wood basket.

of way, and is relatively impermeable. Unless you're planning to trade in salt and beads, nothing will fall through the cracks, an advantage over steel wire baskets.

Sunlite, Paishley, and Nantucket Basket Co. are among other companies producing baskets. And yes, the latter manufactures the iconic basket of baskets, the deep, rounded wicker Nantucket that is perfect for summer weekends when you wish you were at the beach. Basket prices don't always seem logical on first glance. We've seen smaller, seemingly simpler baskets that cost more than larger ones and larger ones that were cheaper than we expected. What we can say is that the more expensive items have higher-quality attachments, better materials, more clever branding, or some combination of the above.

Rear Racks

You'll probably never impress anyone with your rear or front racks the way you can with aesthetic panniers or retro baskets. What are racks but usually some thick steel wire bent to attach efficiently on your bike and create a vertical plane for fastening items, including child seats, cartons, or tennis rackets. But you will have a number of options, and at the higher end, you can find something with style.

Racks attach to your stays in the rear and to the front fork via screws and bolts. They take only a few minutes to install. Many racks come with a spring-activated closing mechanism that will enable you to fasten soft items directly to the rack. It resembles a mousetrap. You will otherwise use straps, string, rope, or, best of all, bungee cords, to secure your stuff. We've also seen cyclists make effective use of Western-style necker-chiefs to create a sort of rear-wheel hobo's bundle. As we've noted, you will also use racks to secure panniers and baskets. They frequently serve as the foundation for improvised crate and cardboard box baskets, and more frequently as seating for passengers. We do not advocate the latter. Nor do rack manu-facturers, although this tradition is unlikely to end.

You can find serviceable racks for under $20 or knock your-self out for more than $200. Germany's Tubus manufactures a

This cargo bike features front and rear racks for extra-big loads.

titanium rear rack that can support 30 kilos, about 65 pounds, and will serve you into the next century when bicycles will fly. The Tubus Carry—surely the company could have thought of a more dynamic name—weighs less than a pound. The price is $260 online with separate bars to allow the rider to attach panniers. A version without the extra pannier bars costs $245. A carbon and aluminum rack costs nearly $200. It can only accommodate a seven-kilo load but includes bungee cords, which will save you a trip to the local mountaineering store. The $177 Old Man Mountain Cold Springs rear rack offers a vertical aluminum plate for steadying objects. But for aesthetics, we particularly admired the Minoura Gamoh, which combines steel wire supports with a base of three vertical wooden slats. It costs less and suggests bike rides through the Maine countryside, although its creator is a publicly traded Japanese company. For front racks, we think highly of Velo Orange's Porteur, a copy of a French bicycle delivery rack. Velo Orange may sound like a French techno pop band but is based in Annapolis, Maryland, the home of the U.S. Naval Academy.

Packing

You've been throwing your stuff into bags for years. Work clothes for business trips. Gym clothes for the health club. Groceries. Home supplies. Aside from ensuring that eggs aren't under the watermelon, glass bottles are at the bottom, and tortilla chips sit open on top for quick snacking, we don't give arrangements much consideration. Packing a bicycle requires a little more thought. That's what Dan Dabrek, the executive director of the Los Angeles bicycle advocacy group CICLE (Cyclists Inciting Change thru Live Exchange), said.

Dabrek has been using the bicycle for transportation for the better part of a decade. He describes himself as "car light," commuting to most business meetings from his home north-east of the city. "When I started cycling more, I found myself enjoying the city more," he said. "I enjoyed the experience of meeting people. When people saw me on the street, they smiled. It passed on a positive message."

CICLE promotes the bicycle as a regular means of trans-portation. Among its services, it offers inexperienced cyclists looking to commute or run errands a course in packing. Dabrek said there's no weight limit, aside from what a frame can accom-modate. Still, he said that if you can't maneuver the bike easily, you're carrying too much weight. "If you don't have control, you have too much on it," Dabrek said. "Then you don't have a good balance, and you're putting yourself in danger."

Among CICLE's packing tips, cyclists should do the following:

- Start with only a few items and gradually work their way to heavier burdens. "It's best to start small and light," Dabrek said.

- Ensure that their baskets and panniers are secure. If they are loaded down and shift, they can upset your balance.

- Pack the heaviest, most durable goods, such as cans and quarts of juice or milk, at the bottom just as you do when packing paper grocery bags. They will help anchor your panniers or baskets. Keep more delicate stuff at the top where they are less likely to be crushed.

- Surround the heavier items with softer ones to immo-bilize them. If heavier items start swaying into empty spaces, you may as well. "We're suggesting that you use something to create a secure or tight space," Dabrek said.

- Allot the most weight to rear holders. If you have too much weight up front, it may inhibit your ability to steer properly.

- Keep errands involving perishable goods to the end of your ride. It's no fun washing a pannier of melted vanilla ice cream.

10

Commuting

How to Survive the Road to Work

So you want to cycle to work?

You're revved up. You've got a good set of wheels. You've made the decision to do something good for yourself and society. You're going to be healthier, reduce your carbon imprint, and serve as a rolling wheeling advocate for returning to the simple things.

Now what?

Our recent urban cycling acquaintance Mark Halliday in the Boston suburb of Arlington says not to rush things.

Say what?

What Halliday means, and he speaks from two decades of bicycle commuting experience, is that you probably won't do everything right the first or the second time. Nor should you try to be perfect because there will always be some scenario—a piece of clothing you forgot, a missing lock, or a breakdown that you can't anticipate.

"Commuting is really about trying out things, going with the flow, not worrying about what happens the first time," said Halliday, a software developer for State Street Financial. "It's an exploration of a way to get from Point A to Point B, an exploration on many levels: clothing, the bike, the route."

It's life. And forgive us if we get all philosophical here, but people who succeed in life don't get discouraged. In bicycle commuting that means treating each mud-splattered work pants leg and every jammed chain with the same equanimity you would a perfect ride on a sunny day. You've made a lifestyle decision with all its advantages—many—and downside—small. Go with it.

You might also take comfort in the Danes. They vie with the Dutch as the world's most bicycling country. In icy winter, snow or rain, they (apologies to literature's most famous Dane, Hamlet) find it nobler in the mind to pedal, perchance to dream of the occasional sunny day in spring. Sometime when you have nothing better to do, find a video of the bicyclists' jamboree that is Copenhagen streets.

Feel inspired.

We do not underestimate the severity of a Boston, New York, Detroit, Chicago, or Denver winter, and certainly not that of Minneapolis. But none have anything on Northern Europe—and we could equally point to the bike-friendly Germans, French, Belgians, and assorted Scandinavians. If such cultures can forge on with bicycles for commuting, then so can you.

Ride a Bicycle to Work?

If you're still hedging about commuting by bicycle, we'd like you to consider the questions below. We will take the liberty of providing the answers. Then you can make your decision.

- Will you be physically healthier? Yes. The advantages of regular exercise in an obese world have been well documented. We're fat. We need to move more, among other things. Bicycling is a particularly excellent option as we discuss in an earlier chapter. You will burn lots of calories, improve your cardiovascular fitness, and do it all without turning various joints to oatmeal.

- Will you be mentally healthier? Yes. We do not just refer to feeling the joys of being active. That's a big part of it, whether you're pedaling hard enough to stimulate endorphins, those feel-good chemicals that you release when you exercise hard, or simply energized by increased blood flow and (we hope) fresh air. "I like to start and end my

Many cities offer resources for long-distance commuters who combine public transportation and cycling.

days with fresh air and exercise," said Mark Halliday. We mean the ability to unwind, to separate from the connected world. Downtime is thinking time. We watch *Mad Men*. We've seen the mad advertising genius Don Draper prone on his couch, pondering. Today we'd put him in a pair of khakis and have him admiring the leaves, breathing deeply, and creating from the saddle.

- Will you be happier? Yes. We've sort of answered this one already in our point directly above. But let's draw out the logic. If you feel better physically and you're functioning at a higher level mentally, you will be more pleasant and productive. Everyone will like you more. That includes your boss, who will pay you increasingly large sums of money to do what you do. That means that he or she will pay you to think more, which means you will have to make the big sacrifice of riding your bicycle more. You will be paid to ride a bicycle.

- Will you be helping the environment? Yes. Here's where we could cite all sorts of statistics from all sorts of groups that go by their acronyms. Do we need to? If you're not driving a car as often, you'll be using less gas, which means you'll be sending fewer toxic waste products into the air. The oil companies will have less to do, which means they'll be sending fewer toxic waste products into the air and sea. You'll also be creating a lesser market for car and motorcycle manufacturers, which means they will need to produce fewer parts and therefore expend less energy in manufacturing and shoot fewer toxic waste products into the air. And if the car and motorcycle industries are producing fewer cars, that means their suppliers will be cutting back and shooting fewer toxic waste products into the air. You will also be happier and smile more. Your personal glow will make the animals and birds in the forest, not to mention your fellow humans, happier. You will be brightening the environment.

- Will you look cool? Yes. Do you want to be a wildebeest? You know, those African creatures who look like a cross between a steer and Jeff Bridges in *True Grit*? (We are great fans of Jeff Bridges, but liked the original *Grit* more.) Wildebeest run the plains of the Serengeti in huge waves, the better to ensure that enough of them make it to mating season. Individualists they are not. If you prefer this lifestyle—the old and weak get picked off by assorted lionesses and Mara River crocodiles—stay in your car. If you'd rather lead the way, instead of following the pack, get your helmet and get going. Bicyclists represent the new. We think setting trends is much cooler than monitoring them. Be singular. Be the lion. Be cool.

- Will you save money? Yes and double-yes. At the time of this writing, gas was topping $4 per gallon. One of us recently filled the family Suburu for a personal-record $60. Multiply that for a monthly gas tab and you're speaking real money for a middle-class family. Don't remind us of the rising cost of new tires, maintenance, insurance, and, in cities, parking garages. We know of one New York City parking garage on 48th Street between 1st and 2nd Avenues that costs about $450 per month. And forgive us if we mention California's new and improved fines for parking and driving violations while cursing under our breath. Park in a bus, loading or disabled parking zone and you're out almost $1,000.

Getting Started

We hesitate to use the expression, but this isn't rocket science. You'll start with a bicycle. Many of you will already have something in the garage. It's probably a bike you've used sporadically or kept with the spoken promise that you'd take up riding regularly to live healthier. It may need some tinkering to get it into commuting shape.

A hardhat-wearing commuter heads in to work on Portland's Swan Island, his materials for the day stored in a front basket. No matter your profession, part of planning your commute is determining how to transport what you need to bring with you. (J. MAUS/BIKEPORTLAND)

Remember the bike store down the street you've been passing? It's time for a visit. We outline the fundamentals for a tune-up in our maintenance section. If you are one of those who donated your last bike to Goodwill, we direct you to the virtual shopping center of shopping centers—Craigslist—or a bike shop. And don't be worried about what other people think. Hybrid, mountain, touring, city bike, little BMX—that would be odd in a business suit—if they work well, they'll get you where you want to go.

You'll need a bag for comfortably storing your work, a laptop, foul-weather clothing, and possibly a change of clothes and shoes. If you prefer to wear less weight, you may instead wish to invest in panniers, bike saddle bags, a rack, and/or a front basket. The trio of accoutrements can be helpful if you stop regularly at the grocery store on your way home.

Everyone has a preference. Los Angeles cycling commuter Jonathan West favors a black messenger bag he wears expertly across his chest. Some people complain that these bags, which have become popular in recent years, swing around, upsetting their balance. West's bag seems to barely move. Kelly Martin of Los Angeles' Bike Kitchen uses a rear rack and backpack. Halliday prefers the backpack approach. It gives him more room for his gear and work things. We'll offer more on the subject of accessories later on.

Picking Your Route

Let's pretend that it's Monday morning in your new life as a bicycle commuter. You've downed a farewell cup of coffee. The messenger bag/backpack/panniers are packed. You're ready to go. But where? Oh, we know that you know your final destination—the office hasn't moved since Friday.

A cyclist leaves the bike path along the Los Angeles River.

The question is what's the best way to get there? If your car commute depends on highways, you may not be able to bike the way you drive. Or you may be safer avoiding boulevards. Four- and six-lane arteries, even with traffic lights, can be no less appropriate for bike traffic than the freeway. Fortunately, you'll always have a choice.

We will now ask you to return to the evening before your first bike commute. Unless you're new to the city or don't venture out much, you'll probably be familiar with the surrounding streets. Still, a little strategizing is in order. Find a street plan online. Some urban biking groups and nongovernmental agencies highlight bike friendly roads. Then consider your options. Most commuters face one basic choice: speedy and direct or an approach that bypasses major thoroughfares for smaller, quieter streets? Halliday is invigorated by scenery, so goes slightly out of his way to follow the Charles River. The executive, Henry Gold, who's been commuting for years in Toronto may detour to pass food shops where he can put together meals for himself and

Bike paths sometimes run along busy freeways.

his wife. Gold's company, Tour d'Afrique, assembles multiweek bike tours, often through developing nations.

Back to the next morning: your directions may work ideally. Via a route plotted for speed, you may arrive only marginally later than you would have by car. In his postcompetitive days, former Olympic cyclist Ron Skarin used to take pride in passing cars on Los Angeles' jam-packed Sepulveda Boulevard as he made the 10-mile commute to his job as a building inspector with the city. "You used to see the people's faces as they had to sit in traffic while I just flew by," Skarin said. You may find inner peace taking a longer route along tree-lined streets where traffic is light—or not. Finding routes you like is trial and error and part of the commuting adventure.

Halliday charted his Charles River path after looking for something more poetic than a straight dose of city streets. Gold experimented for years and now chooses from a number of possible routes to travel the two or three miles from his home to office. "It's trial and error," Halliday said.

Counting the Blinking Lights

Momentum is such a key to bicycling that most cyclists will do anything to make sure that their feet never touch the ground and their pedals never stop moving. There are several reasons for wanting to maintain your momentum—from arriving at your destination faster to maintaining your position in traffic. But mostly it's because coming to a complete stop for a few seconds before resuming your ride wastes energy, time, and, for some, patience. That is why many cyclists illegally run red lights or stop signs, go the wrong way on one-way streets, or cycle in a circle at the edge of a crosswalk waiting for the light to change. For many cyclists, putting your foot down on the street at any time is a sign that you're a novice—a better cyclist would have foreseen the red light a block earlier and timed his approach so that he caught the green light and was able to proceed nonstop.

There is no premonition for knowing when the light is going to change.

You just need to know how to count.

One of the best—and legal—ways to keep your momentum is to time the lights so that you know how long you have until the red light turns green.

"Using the crosswalk lights is an awesome trick I use all the time," said Bill Jackson, a daily bicycling commuter for more than 10 years. "Just don't get so fixated with looking off to the side at them that you hit a pothole, or worse."

Advanced street lights have a countdown for how long pedestrians have to cross the street. However, those light systems only represent a fraction of all the intersections in any city. More often than not, you will encounter traditional stoplights that only tell pedestrians if they can WALK or DON'T WALK and blink the DON'T WALK sign until the light changes. The number of times that the DON'T WALK sign blinks will change from intersection to intersection so this trick requires memory.

But if you take the same commute to work each day or the same roads to wherever you go, you can learn how long each intersection will give you before the light changes. A bicyclist who is paying attention and looking for this can watch the lights a block ahead and start counting how many times a sign has blinked.

If you know a given intersection will blink 12 times before the green light turns red, then you will know how many seconds you have to get through an intersection so that your ride can continue unimpeded.

For example, one of the authors commutes daily from Chicago's Wrigleyville to the South Loop along Broadway and Clark streets. Once the commute has crossed Division Street going south, traffic starts getting more congested, and the approach to each intersection has to be timed to keep moving forward without stopping. Years of doing the same commute have honed the ability to memorize the light sequences for a key stretch of the commute.

The combination for getting through the street lights along southbound Clark Street between Division and Grand streets is: 15-10-15-10-10-20-10-10-12-15.

What that means is that after crossing Division Street, we know that the next street light will blink for 10 seconds at Elm St., 15 seconds at Maple St., 10 seconds at Oak St., 20 seconds at Chicago, 10 seconds at Superior, and so on. Like a scene from an *Indiana Jones* movie, a cyclist will find each street light silently obeying his inner wishes and turning green at the perfect moment if the cyclist speeds up or slows down according to the time allowed between each intersection.

But this trick is only applicable if you want to keep your feet from ever touching the ground. If that doesn't matter to you or if you're looking for a better workout from your ride, then stopping at each intersection is better for you. After all, the best workout your legs will get on your ride is primarily the burst you have to generate from a dead stop at every red light.

"I use the acceleration from the light as a way to get a good workout," Jackson said, who prefers to get the most exercise from his ride, not the quickest time. "I don't [count lights] to preserve momentum. I look at lights to know when to stop."

That brings us to an important by-product of bike travel. You'll learn more about your city than you ever could driving a car. On a commute through Glendale and Hollywood last December with Jonathan West, we spied coffeehouses and restaurants on streets we'd whizzed through for years. Where did they come from? Many had clearly been in their locations for years. And we found a block of nearly century-old craftsmen homes wedged between the 101 freeway and an area of urban blight. A neighbor, Matthew Butterick, took us over Mount Hollywood to a place with maybe the best breakfast burritos in Los Angeles—and we've sampled a few in our day. We'd been passing the hole-in-the-wall for years without noticing the lines in front.

Commuting can be your own Discovery Channel.

What Do You Do If You Break Down?

You've done all the right things for months. You're feeling good and then, in the words of celebrity chef Emeril Lagasse, "Bam." The tire pops. The chain jams horribly. Something unwelcome occurs. We are not worried that you will figure out a way to address the situation. Undoubtedly after reading our maintenance chapter, you will have your trusty tool, or on the off chance that you forget your tool bag, you will nurse your bike to your shop for repairs. Rather, we worry about how this will affect your commitment. Repairs for the inexperienced take time, and when that happens interest wanes and your car with seat warmers, a nice cupholder for your coffee, and FM radio looks very, very inviting. *You know, I have a meeting to prepare for, my hands are cold, I'll walk my bike to work, take the bus home, and leave it for the repair shop over the weekend.*

Our response: it's Monday, five days from the weekend. DON'T PROCRASTINATE!"

We would suggest that breakdowns are the perfect opportunity to demonstrate your allegiance to your new lifestyle. Set things right quickly. Get back on your bike.

How to Handle an Angry Pedestrian

Bike long enough and you'll have a problem with a pedestrian. Usually it's an accident that happens because both of you have made a mistake. One of you loses focus and zigs into the other's path, or some variation on the theme. On many of these occasions, the pedestrian matadors out of the way, or you swerve at the last second and both move on unscathed with a shouted "sorry" or "excuse me" trailing in the wind.

But occasionally, you'll face someone who has it in for bikes. We can't imagine why, although there are also people who don't like puppies and kittens. Perhaps, like the Grinch, this individual's heart is three sizes too small. Anyway, these folks not only won't share space with cyclists, but may seek confrontation. Mark Halliday's nemesis is the owner of two golden retrievers. You'd think anyone owning the world's friendliest family dog would love cyclists. But this individual screams at bicyclists as they pass on a path to the Charles River. Halliday has tried to keep a distance but also resorted to keeping a record of the confrontations. "My intention is to ask where his anger comes from," Halliday said. We suggest a similar approach. There's no place for road rage in cycling.

What to Wear, What to Bring, Final Checklist

You will unquestionably have your own checklist for commuting. Perhaps there's a lucky charm you bring everywhere, or you have to change socks at work. We like to have tissues for our perpetually runny nose and dental floss in our backpack. Still, we felt it would be more helpful than saying about packing, "It's up to you," so we asked longtime commuters what they bring. We wanted at least one of these veterans to come from an area of changing seasons and weather patterns. We figured someone planning for these extremes would have a near-perfect checklist of essentials.

Mark Halliday started commuting by bicycle in 1991. He was living in the Primrose section of London and looking for a more pleasant commute downtown to his job as a developer of interactive CD-ROMs. Parts of his half-hour ride snaked along London's ancient canals. He was hooked and continued his bike commuting ways upon moving to Boston. His commute now takes 35 minutes via his usual Charles River route—about 10 miles one way—and 5 to 10 minutes shorter if he pedals exclusively through the streets—about 8½ miles. He rides a Cannondale Cyclocross bike with racing handlebars and front shocks. He's vigilant about keeping his chain clean

Bar Ends and Ear Buds Can Kill You

She stood 5'4" and weighed no more than 110 pounds dripping wet, but she left me bleeding worse than any man, woman, animal, pothole, or cab driver ever has. I look down at my permanently scarred left pinky and ring finger and remember a lesson anew every time—bar ends and ear buds can hurt you if you are not careful.

It was a great spring morning, and I was cycling to work along Chicago's famous lakefront bike path. When the path becomes part of Lower Wacker Drive where Lake Shore Drive crosses the Chicago River, it narrows to a wide sidewalk for a few hundred yards.

She was jogging on the right of the path ahead of me, her light brown ponytail bouncing rhythmically. Naturally, I was cycling faster than she was jogging so as I came up behind her I said aloud the standard passing phrase: "On your left." She continued jogging with no acknowledgement. So I repeated myself even louder because I saw she was listening to ear buds. "On your left!" She never heard me. As I pulled next to her, she turned to jog back in the direction we had just come. Her pumping arms and hands knocked me off balance.

but doesn't mind if his frame looks dirty because he believes that a dirty frame discourages thieves. He rode exclusively smooth, hybrid-style tires, but about four years ago when he had a couple of near-accidents on frosty patches, he decided to change to thick studded tires for winter. Here's Halliday's list of commuting essentials:

Bicycle: Very important for bicycle commuting.

Vented helmet: Important for keeping your brains in your skull while not sweating too much.

Bag: Important for holding rain gear and changes of clothes.

Rain gear: Important for keeping dry.

I went flying with only the concrete barricades stopping me. I went from 13 mph to full stop in a matter of 50 blood-streaked feet.

There was fault on both sides.

My error was having my hands solely on the bar ends. Without keeping them over the brake levers, there was no way to stop or slow quickly. Keeping your hands on the ends is more comfortable, but potentially more painful since brakes are not normally installed to coordinate with bar ends.

"Are you all right?" she yelled over the music pumping from the ear buds.

"I said, 'On your left!'" I roared furiously, holding my hand in front of her face, the blood pooling on my handlebars and shoes. "Can't you hear me?"

"I didn't hear you," she said weakly, turning down the volume.

The injury was "merely a flesh wound," to quote the film *Monty Python and the Holy Grail*. There were no broken bones or bike parts so I calmed myself for the final three miles of my commute.

The lesson from this incident is simple—never cycle using solely your bar ends if anyone is nearby. But the bigger lesson is that using ear buds makes you a danger to yourself and others.

Will she remember her mistake? Doubtful. When she jogged away, she reset her ear buds as if nothing had happened.

—S.R.

Tool kit: Very important for making repairs.

Bungy cords for the rear rack: Very important for securing the bag with spare clothes and work.

Water bottle: Very important when Boston is sweltering in the summer. Depending on where you live, drink from public fountains at your own risk.

Lock: Very important for ensuring you'll have a bike with which to commute home. Halliday once had a bike stolen in front of Harvard University, of all places. He prefers a Kryptonite Fahgettaboutit chain, very strong and very heavy.

Work clothes and shoes: What's the point of bicycle commuting if you don't have dry, presentable work clothes and shoes without clips?

11

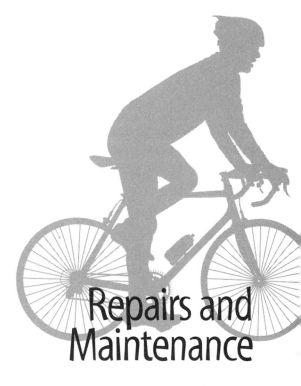

Repairs and Maintenance

How to Survive by Taking Better Care of Your Bike

Nuts and Bolts…and a Little More

Most of us don't really need to know how something works to enjoy it. You don't ponder the steer when tucking into sirloin, and you don't dwell over plumbing mechanics.

As long as our wheels propel us and the steering and brakes keep us from killing ourselves, we're mostly blissfully ignorant about our bikes. Mechanical problems? We turn to the local bike shop or friends who have bike shops in their basements. Those seeking higher truths of bike anatomy will find ample resources on the Internet and in print to satisfy their cravings. There are Web videos to teach you how to grease ball bearings and build a frame—but do not count us as advocates for doing either yourself. We list a number of bike maintenance websites that we admire in this book's final chapter.

Yet between the extremes of helpless junkie and grease monkey, a little knowledge of components and maintenance can help you keep your bike in good shape longer and ease the occasional quick repair. You'll also impress the local bike shop owner, friends, neighbors, and relatives.

Bicycles aren't complicated. Georgena Terry, the pioneering women's bicycle manufacturer, needs fewer than 10 minutes to explain design in a YouTube video. Terry uses nothing more than an artist's sketchpad and magic marker. Think moving erector sets, something Hasbro could box with instructions for a young scientists' movement. You have tubes, wheels, a chain, a few metal plates, a coil here and there, ball bearings, grease, a seat, some plastic, and rubber accoutrements. Add nuts and bolts, a few welds (perhaps the Hasbro set shouldn't come with a blowtorch), and a dash of adhesive (grips and reflectors) for assembly.

Were you to build a bicycle from scratch, the instructions for assembly would start with a frame, usually crafted of aluminum or steel tubing about the circumference of a silver dollar (mountain bikes and hybrids) or quarter (road bikes). Some fancy road bikes are made of carbon fiber or titanium. Three of these tubes, welded together, form a central triangle. This is the bicycle's foundation and for good reason.

As our geometry teachers explained, the triangle is particularly stable, the basis of truss bridges strong enough to support freight trains and many high-rise buildings. A second, smaller triangular shape of thinner, semiflat tubes extends behind the seat, brackets the rear wheel, and provides structural support for the bike's transmission—read chain and gearing systems. A front, or so-called head tube, angles almost 90 degrees from the top two sides of the main triangle and serves as a foundation for the front wheel and steering components—stem and handlebars. Another shorter, narrower tube, the seat post, will lead to your saddle. Your bike skeleton is largely in place. We'd like to say that bike-building pioneers knew immediately that the diamond construction was strongest, but it took decades of tinkering before they hit upon the right design. Even then, it took a few years of refinements before society had bikes that resemble our modern versions.

We'll call your brakes "part two" of your assembly instructions. Start with the cables that extend from levers on your handlebars. Thread them through synthetic sleeves called housing to brake pads. These are metal clamps with rubber insets on the front and rear wheels. The left lever powers the rear brakes and offers the most control over your stopping. The right lever manages the front brakes. Use it solely and abruptly as we've done unintentionally on a couple of occasions, and you'll fly over the handlebars. In Olympic diving, that's a 9.5 score for a full gainer with a twist.

Part three: your transmission and gearing involves a series of toothy, circular plates, cranks, cables, and pedals with a chain at the core. Think of a shinier, small-scale version of the industrial machinery grinding in Charlie Chaplin's masterpiece *Modern Times*. An accident? Chaplin's factory portrayed technology whose roots extended into the nineteenth century when Western civilization mastered the mass production of steel.

The chain connects to a chain ring and a cassette, which looks like a stack of jagged CDs, and attaches to the rear wheel. When you click the right shifter on your handlebars, a rear derailleur, a pulley and spring device (encased in a pinky-sized covering), changes the position of the chain. This allows you to climb hills or increase velocity with greater ease. Click the

saddle

seatpost

seatpost binder bolt

top tube

seatstay

rear brake

cassette

rear dropout

derailleur

chain rings

chain

chainstay

handlebar

shift lever

brake cable

stem

headset

head tube

front brake

fork

pedal

crank arm

hub

spoke

tire

rim

left shifter and you adjust the position of the chain on the chain ring via a front derailleur. The effect on your driving is similar. The derailleur is one of those wonderful innovations born of necessity. Next time you're puffing up a steep incline, say a big merci to Frenchman Paul de Vivie, who in 1905 created a derailleur for shifting the bike chain over toothy cogs as he looked for ways to navigate the hills near his home in Southern France. De Vivie's operated four gears.

You'll build the wheels from metal or composite (very expensive) rims with spokes and a rubber tube and tread. The spokes maintain tension, ensuring the rim doesn't collapse. Add a seat and you're set to roll—panniers, racks, baskets, and fenders optional. We won't quiz you at the end of this chapter, but if you want to learn what to call what, consider the accompanying glossary and diagram of a city bike on the previous page. Mountain bikes with elaborate dual-shock and suspension systems possess a somewhat different list of components.

Of course, we simplify. But our point is that for a gadget that can reach speeds of more than 50 mph on downhills if you're a Tour de France racer or late for a meeting, there are relatively few parts. None of these are of a nature that would require an engineering degree to comprehend. Indeed, these days many hipsters don't bother with gears or brakes. Many consider themselves purists. They like the idea that they are controlling every aspect of their cycling experience and must not depend on gearing and braking systems. No-brake riders stop by ceasing to pedal. The added benefit of these bicycles is that riders can balance on their pedals as they wait at stoplights—that is, if they decide to stop at stoplights. Need we say that most no-brake riders are maverick, casual in their approach to intersections? Some of our urban cycling friends use stronger language, including *reckless* and *anarchistic*. We prefer a more diplomatic approach. We like brakes. We like them very much on the steep hills around Griffith Park where Lance Armstrong occasionally trained in his Sheryl Crow–dating days. We like them in San Francisco—duh. We like them in Denver, Salt Lake City, Flagstaff, Albuquerque, Santa Fe, and on softer slopes around Dallas. We also like them for busy intersections in Miami Beach, Philadelphia, Washington D.C., and New York, among other places, and for avoiding drivers who do not look kindly on cyclists or open their car doors without looking. We like gears, too. We use them on hills, particularly when we're lugging a backpack full of work and workout clothes.

It's not that we don't advocate the fixed-gear approach. We believe that fixie riders look way cool, particularly when they've outfitted their bikes with metallic-colored, five-spoke wheels. We recently admired a train of fixies with fuscia and lime-green hubs on Los Angeles' famed Sunset Boulevard. One of the most wonderful parts of biking is that you can do things your own way as long as you're not endangering anyone. It is the supreme individualist's sport.

The urban practitioner is frequently the freest of spirits.

Common Maladies and Solutions

Few urban cyclists will never tackle a major repair project at home. Larger repairs require time, space, and expertise, all in short supply for busy urbanites. *Where in my 300-square-foot studio apartment can I keep the truing wheel? Ouch, was that a multitool and wrench under my pillow?* Repair shops are an easier option and less expensive when you figure your own per-hour pay.

But you'll save yourself long walks home by learning how to tackle a few common, emergency fix-its—jammed chains, bent rims, broken spokes, and flat tires. Not that we would discourage anyone with self-help inclinations and some room from unleashing their inner mechanic. We know several people who find therapy in tinkering with their bikes. Los Angeles-based Jonathan West enjoys the experience so much that he volunteers Tuesdays at the Bike Kitchen, a nonprofit organization that teaches riders—largely low-income—how to fix their own bikes. West worked in a Washington D.C.–area bike shop years ago before moving to Glendale, an incorporated town in Los Angeles County. He commutes nearly seven miles to his job in a Hollywood art bookstore, another three miles to the Kitchen, and returns home after 10 PM on his volunteering days. He is a gentle presence whether it's guiding riders through basic repairs or total construction. During a visit in 2010, we watched him help a young would-be script writer, a recent Los Angeles transplant fed up with Hollywood parking restrictions, adjust the derailleur on a bicycle he'd built from scratch with West. By January, the scriptwriter would be pedaling a 20-something gear, steel-frame road bike down Hollywood Boulevard. Sometimes West's jobs are more profoundly important. The Kitchen is surrounded by some of Los Angeles' poorest, most troubled neighborhoods. Wheels of any sort mean employment and freedom. "The payoff comes from turning a bad situation to a good one. We get a lot of people down on their luck. They didn't think they could be helped, and we show them how to turn things around, and then they're eternally grateful."

For some people, the fun of having a bicycle is learning how to work with the parts.

Flat Tires

Regardless of whether you're the Whistler's Mother of slow-moving cyclists or have Roger Federer's reflexes, you're bound to hit something tire unfriendly. It's simply impossible to avoid every road crack, pothole, or carpet tack. Indeed, you'll probably hit one while avoiding another. One of us once hit a light pole and bent a rim as he swerved past a hole in the sidewalk. Okay, so he shouldn't have been riding on the sidewalk. But grant us our point. At some time, you'll find yourself with a bum tire miles from home. Usually it will occur in a driving rainstorm when you have no rain gear and the only shelter is a palm tree missing half its fronds. As you march your wounded bicycle miles homeward, you may find yourself swearing new allegiance to covered transportation. "Punctures are one of the factors that people cite most frequently as a good reason not to cycle to work," writes London-based uber-mechanic Mel Allwood in *The Complete Do-It-Yourself Bike Book*, a reader-friendly guide to bike maintenance, etiquette, and safety.

Allwood is one of those cycling experts of unlikely background and deep-rooted passion. She started working in a local bike co-op in the South London community of Brixton, attended Cambridge before returning to her first love, bicycles, and is now the author of five bike maintenance books. Allwood knows her way around a spoke wrench—the tool for tightening and loosening spokes—but in the *Do-It-Yourself Bike Book*, Allwood writes with a simple clarity that's encouraging but not patronizing for novice cyclists. We know few people more in love with what they do than cyclists. "We don't cycle because we're virtuous," writes Allwood. "We do it because we smile."

The much admired bicycling/social commentator Bicycle Snob, the former book publisher Eben Weiss, may not smile as much outwardly. But he also possesses strong feelings about flats. In his 2010 book *Bike Snob: Systematically & Mercilessly Realigning the World of Cycling,* he writes that every school child should be required to learn how to fix a tire "instead of teaching them worthless stuff like auto shop, finger painting, and 'math.'"

We urban cyclists draw the line at finger painting, a profoundly important activity in cultivating creative minds. But Bike Snob has a point. Tire repair is a point of practicality. You'll save yourself a lot of trouble and enhance your biking experience by figuring out the basics.

Tire failure involves the inner tube, the inflatable ring between the metal rim and the treaded exterior layer. This inner tube as much as any bicycle innovation was responsible for popularizing bicycles in the late nineteenth century. Invented by the Scotch veterinarian John Dunlop in 1888 as he sought improvements for his son's tricycle, it largely addressed the problem of comfort. Dunlop found that tires filled with compressed air create a smoother ride and enable

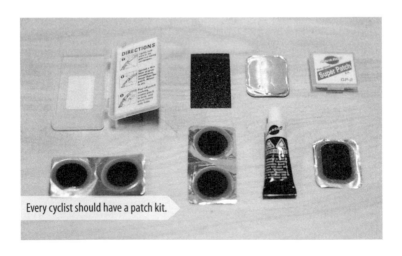

Every cyclist should have a patch kit.

the bicyclist to go faster. Three short years later, the French company Michelin improved on the Dunlop invention, creating a detachable tire that could be more easily changed or repaired. Before the so-called pneumatic tire, people rode on wooden or metal rims. Cycling was not for the weak of bottom.

In the classic flat tire, a sharp object punctures the tread and tube and the tire loses pressure quickly. But tires may also deflate quickly when an object lodges between the rim and rubber. This is known as a snakebite piercing, so-called because the holes appear to have been made by fangs. More subtle tube damage may stem from worn tires. Air will leak slowly. You'll pedal harder and harder to travel the same distance, sort of like trying to move in a bowl of oatmeal. Regardless of severity, avoid riding on rails. Rims and spokes are not meant for the brunt of human weight.

Your first foray may take a while, but the repair process isn't difficult. Most how-to repair texts offer similar variations on a theme. A patch kit should be part of a small tool bag that you carry whenever you ride. (See the "What to Bring" passage for a list of tool bag options.) The patch kit includes a spare tube, glue, and an air pump.

Dismount, turn the bike upside down, remove the tire, repair the inner tube or replace it, and reinflate the tire. "Once you know what you're doing, it's not a long process," said Jonathan West. We'll direct you to the real experts at Bicycling. com, BikeForums.com, and SheldonBrown.com for a more in-depth blow-by-blow.

Dare we admit that we have occasionally forgotten to replace a spare tube in our tool kit? Yes, but only to make the point that there are homespun remedies to get you home. And we do not mean by carrying your bike to a nearby bus stop. Kelly

Martin, the director of the Bike Kitchen, said you can attach a folded dollar bill or similarly stiff piece of paper to the inside of your tire. It will prevent, or at least retard, air from leaking. "You have to be improvisational," Martin said.

We would be remiss not to highlight flat prevention. Mel Atwood offers a fine, common-sense list in *The Complete Do-It-Yourself Bike Book*. They match or dovetail with recommendations from a wide variety of experts and do not necessitate much effort. Mostly, they require common sense. Atwood's suggestions include the following:

- Keeping your tires inflated to recommended levels. Firm tires may allow you to roll over objects that would pierce soft ones. You'll find a pressure range stamped on the tire sidewalls. Use a bike pump and gauge. Car pumps aren't as accurate because they're designed to fill tires with much greater volumes.

- Replacing tires that have lost much of their thread or seem badly scarred. The thinner the tire, the more susceptible it is to damage.

Find the tire style and rim design you like best.

- Inspecting your tires regularly for tiny sharp objects that may lodge in the threads and bore deeper into the surface if not removed.

- Checking sidewalls for "cuts and splits."

- Riding away from curbs where debris collects.

- Considering puncture-resistant tires or tubes prefilled with sealant. Two warnings though: puncture-resistant tires aren't failproof, and prefilled tubes will only work with small holes.

- Using the largest-diameter tires that will fit on your wheel and frame if you carry a lot of weight regularly.

Jammed or Broken Chain

A jammed chain may result from a chain or chain ring becoming caked with dirt or wearing down. Full stop for definitions: the chain ring, as we mentioned earlier, looks like a stack of CDs with serrated edges. The chain is the chain, roughly the same piece that's been propelling bikes since Grover Cleveland was president. (Trick question: who preceded and followed Cleveland? Answer: Benjamin Harrison, Chester Arthur, and William McKinley; Cleveland served two nonconsecutive terms.) Both the caked and worn chain and chain ring are easy to spot unless you're on a bike with internal gearing—chain ring and other gearing parts covered. In this case, skim.

The jammed chain may also stem from an overexcited rear derailleur (down boy!) pushing the chain into angles and places it shouldn't normally go. Time for a more in-depth definition of the derailleur: it is the little spring-activated piece that attaches to your rear wheel and vaguely resembles a Bluetooth headset. The derailleur pushes your chain diagonally up and

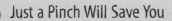

Just a Pinch Will Save You

Next time you start to bonk on your ride, before reaching for an energy bar you might want to reach for your rear tire.

One of the most common maintenance practices is making sure you have proper inflation of your tires. It's the easiest thing to do and also one of the hardest to remember. It may be because it's so easy that many riders forget to keep track of their tire pressure.

We have noticed over the past few years that when we start to feel tired on long rides or commutes, the problem isn't better eating habits but remembering to check tire pressure. The next time you feel tired on a ride sooner than you expected, it might not be lack of energy that is vexing you but the fact that you're riding on underinflated tires.

The friction that the added surface area creates is deceptive and has a way of sneaking up on you. For the first mile or two, you will likely feel that you had a bad day or aren't feeling right, but you will convince yourself that you will snap out of it. When the condition continues for several miles, you will get frustrated and the ride will lose its appeal as it soon is no longer as enjoyable as it was that morning or maybe the day before.

To avoid the beginnings of a flat tire, before you get on your bike just do one simple test while you're strapping on your helmet: pinch your tire.

Grab your rear tire between your thumb and forefinger and pinch it hard. If you can feel the tire give way slightly, you need to inflate your tires. You should not be able to pinch your tires at all. Pinching a correctly inflated tire will feel as solid as pinching a stick in the yard.

Test your front tire the same way. Realize that the front tire will not affect your ride as much as your rear tire will because all of your weight is on the rear tire. In fact, your front tire can be grossly under inflated and you may not notice a difference in your ride. But a slight deflation in the rear tire can completely change your daily ride. Your tires should always be properly inflated. When you finish inflating your tires you will notice the difference in the first 20' of your ride.

Before you question your eating habits or fill your backpack with energy bars, check the tire pressure. You may find that the problem is not you.

down the chain ring enabling you to shift gears—higher for climbing hills, lower for allowing the bike to generate more thrust.

When the chain jams, you face the frustrating sensation of not being able to pedal a full rotation. Your thrust becomes a half thrust until you lose momentum, and you're stuck like a sailboat without wind. As is the case with the flat, this always seems to happen in the middle of a fierce gale on one of the city's busiest thoroughfares. A strange grinding sound usually precedes the jam as cars whiz by you at ever-alarming proximity and speed.

There are occasions when you'll be able to overcome a jam through sheer will—the *I will not let this occur* approach. Curse like a marine and rotate the pedals forward and back with force, but not too vigorously. You may be able to right the chain. On the other hand, too much fortissimo may lead to a more severe jam or even damage your bike. Frankly, you could say the same thing for any sort of repair. The bicycle may be an inanimate object, but like living creatures it responds better to love than harshness.

If the repair-while-riding method doesn't work, you'll have to dismount and use your hands. Pull back on the chain and away from the chainstay and chain ring. If the jam persists, reverse the pedals while you're pulling the chain. Still snagging? Perhaps there's something more serious afoot, a piece of cloth or other object you'll need to untangle. Analyze the problem and go slow.

Broken chain? They take more time to repair. But like most bike repairs, this one doesn't require extreme technical know-how or hours to complete. Here's where you'll need a chain tool, which you'll naturally be carrying in your handy tool bag. Chain tools look something like fancy corkscrews. They allow you to stabilize the chain and slide out the small pins connecting individual links. Remove the damaged links, replace them with extras you're carrying in your tool bag, and you're good to go. What? No extra links? In many cases, you can simply shorten the chain by connecting healthy links.

Malfunctioning Brakes

Riding with malfunctioning brakes is, to say the least, disconcerting. It's not just that you can't stop the way you want to but also a loss of faith in the universe's unwritten guarantee to protect you until scientists figure out cryogenics. Brakes are your security blanket. Expressed mathematically, brake malfunction means increased likelihood of an accident means bad news for whatever part of your body hits the hard, hard road. The good news: if you have your trusty Allen keys, you can make adjustments on the fly. You'll need to find the small screws that help secure the brake clamps and pads on either side of your wheels. Turn them gently one way or the other until the brakes respond suitably to your touch on the hand levers. You don't want to squeeze way down. Nor do you want the brakes so tight that the slightest touch threatens to send you into orbit. With a quick, firm but not overly firm contraction, brakes should stop you efficiently.

MINOR ISSUES THAT ARE SO MINOR WE HESITATE TO MENTION THEM

Keeping the Kickstand Tight

While kickstands may look ungainly or uncool to some or raise foolish concerns about extra weight—how can you argue over a few extra ounces when you're using a bike to pick up three gallons of milk—many urban cyclists hold a more practical attitude toward them. Many are already riding stand-up style hybrids, Dutch-flavored city cycles, or recycled gizmos. These bikes' charm is in their retro qualities. That's retro when kickstands were de rigeur on every brand-leading Schwinn, Raleigh, and Columbia. For them, the kickstand is freedom, freedom to use both hands to lock or unlock your bike, pack your panniers with a laptop and legal pads, or take a call from your Hollywood agent. It's freedom to park your bike in your garage without worrying the next time you reach for a roll of paper towels that it will slam you in the shins.

Practically speaking, those benefits outweigh the cool of streamlining. The kickstand is easily attached via screw and bolt and therefore susceptible with time to loosening. Slack kickstands are deceptive: they may perform for a while until one day your bike falls unexpectedly with the kickstand waving around like a shudder in the wind. We know of one Rockhopper that suffered a bad case of the scratches to its chainstay, the bottom tube anchoring the transmission. The scratches didn't impede bike propulsion, but they marred an otherwise immaculate paint job. We figure that if you're going to shell out the money, why not keep the bike looking good as long as possible?

Tighten the kickstand. Kickstands bracket the chainstay. You may need a screwdriver to hold one side in place while you wrench the bolt tight. If the whole process doesn't sound like much, it isn't.

Unclean Chain and Frame

Bicycles are meant to get dirty. In some camps this is a matter of pride. Dirty bikes among mountain bikers and cyclo-crossers mean they've been tackling trails with enough slop to satisfy their wild side. Some urban bikers, usually fixed-gear riders or veteran commuters, see dirt as a badge of honor. Their logic: a dirty bike is a used bike. Who cares if it's glowing like new? There are those also who say that dirt is a good way to discourage thieves; they're less likely to steal something that's scruffy. Indeed, we know ardent bike people who mess up their bikes intentionally to help protect them from theft. They aerosol paint them and add the random mark. They'd sooner apply some wash to the frame than corrosive acid.

We will address the bike wash later in our section on the tune-up. Suffice it to say here that particularly in dusty areas or cold communities where roads break down and salt and grit are common, the strategic bike bath can help prevent equipment breakdown. If you're riding a steel frame, it can also prolong the life of your bike. Keep to a regular schedule, and you'll spend no more than five or 10 minutes per washing. Adopt a looser approach, and dirt will accumulate. That's particularly true for the chain and rear-wheel cassette with eventual consequences for gearing and the smoothness of your ride.

Chain care is an important part of bike maintenance.

We hesitate to say that you'll need a soft cloth. An old towel, T-shirt, or dish rag will do. If you want to get fancy, try some microfiber sheets at $20-plus per pack. Several manufacturers of bike tools sell individual brushes or sets with sizes addressing different parts of the bike. On Amazon.com, we recently saw a four-brush Parktools set and five-brush Pedro's package for $17 and $19, respectively. The brushes included long and short, soft and harder bristles, brushes not much larger than mascara liners, and others shaped like crab claws and pinecones. But you can do perfectly well and lessen your carbon footprint with old toothbrushes, hairbrushes, and boot brushes, or even real mascara liners.

You'll want to use a degreaser for the chain. The major bike maintenance companies and others carry similar and competing formulas in a variety of colors and bottles. Degreasers will help remove the smallest grit from chains before you apply lube. But they are harder on paint.

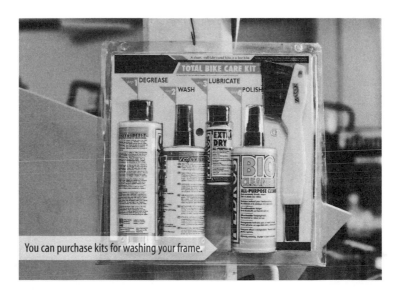

You can purchase kits for washing your frame.

Among bike washes, Finish Line produces a pink-bubble-gum concoction. A liter bottle on REI.com costs $13. Finish Line is one of the industry leaders of bike care products and is easy to find both online and at bike retailers and generalist stores. The unpleasant-sounding Muc-Off offers a wash of similar hue for $12 per liter. Car washes by simple green and homemade solutions of diluted shampoos or soaps coupled with some elbow wax may work equally well and cost less per ounce. On the other hand, stay away from dish soap. It is a stronger solution than other soaps and more apt to break down finishes.

What to Bring

We fall into the minimalist camp. A few tools will address almost all your roadside servicing needs. For a whip list of

Don't Use Police Stickers

There are plenty of ways to ugly up your bike to deter thieves from thinking it looks good to them.

Cyclists use old stickers and duct tape and purposefully never wash the bike or cover scratches to make bikes look worse than they are. They hope these tactics will keep someone from stealing anything from their bike, too. But don't use police stickers to ward off potential thieves.

"We have our bikes stolen too," said a Chicago bicycle officer who didn't want his name used. The officer and his partner said that stickers would be illegal because they suggest that you are impersonating a police officer. But the officers said that the biggest reason not to use police stickers was because "thieves will sometimes look for a police bike to steal. By trying to ward off thieves, you may actually be attracting them."

And here you thought the recurring joke on the now-cancelled Comedy Central series *Reno 911* with Lt. Jim Dangle's bike constantly being stolen was just humorous.

essentials we turned to Los Angeles–based urban cycling advocate Kelly Martin. The 40-year-old Martin is executive director of the repair cooperative, the Bike Kitchen.

Martin spent a good portion of her child and teen years relying on bicycles for transportation—neither of her parents had driver's licenses for years, even after her family settled in the less-than-bike-Mecca of Anchorage, Alaska. At lower latitudes as a college student, she continued to rely on two-wheeled transportation and again in her late twenties and thirties after moving to car-centric Los Angeles. She took her interest a step further when she started volunteering at the Bike Kitchen. Now she oversees the Kitchen's small army of volunteer mechanics, secures parts, and writes grants that keep the Kitchen open. The Kitchen does not charge for its services but works on a donation basis. Many of the shop's clients are lower income. The Bike Kitchen helps ensure they'll have wheels to look for work. Similar models have opened in past

With a few tools, cyclists can maintain their bicycles on the go.

years around the country as more people in cities depend on bikes for transportation. There are now at least five repair co-ops in Los Angeles and its surrounding areas alone. "I guess you could say that it's a movement," Martin said.

Martin knows bike repair, commutes to work, and runs chores by bike. Martin's self-described fool bag holds a multitool, triangle hex wrench, adjustable wrench, tri-flow tire lever for easier tire removal, patch kit, spare tube, and pump. She tucks it into a larger bag that she keeps on her rear rack. The bag itself should be small and lightweight with a zipper or drawstring at the end. If it's waterproof, you'll be even better off. Moisture and tools are not a good match. "It doesn't weigh much and will cover you for just about anything not requiring a massive overhaul," said Martin.

Another longtime Los Angeles bike advocate, repair guru Larry Hoffman, is even more minimalist. Hoffman ran a brisk bicycle servicing business from the North Hollywood bicycle

A good multi-tool is essential.

store he sold in 2005. He said all you need is a multitool set—which depending on the level of quality ranges from a few dollars to more than $40—as well as a patch kit, spare tube, and pump. To prove his point one late autumn afternoon, he used his multitool kit to complete a tune-up on a department store–quality hybrid. As is the case with bicycles bought at large generalist chains, the bicycle had been suffering from a bad case of the loose brakes and cables.

In an informal purchasing study, we found the well-reviewed Ventura multitool with 12 different tools for $6, not including shipping, from the Michigan-based Meijer chain of stores and for roughly double that price online at Walmart, Kmart, and Target. The instrument includes seven Allen keys, a Phillips and flathead screwdriver, a T25 torx tool (otherwise known as a star-shaped screwdriver), a chain rivet extractor, and a cutter. "If there's something really complicated or serious you're going to take it in," Hoffman said. "Just about everything else you can take care of with just the basics."

Of course, we are sure there are a few type-A cyclists who don't feel right unless they're carting a wider assortment of tools. We hope that we're riding with them the next time we suffer a major breakdown. How you prepare, like just about everything else related to bicycle riding, is a matter of preference.

A Final Note: Lube

We will state the obvious. Lube keeps your chain functioning smoothly and you would be wise to reapply it regularly. With time, even in ideal riding conditions, lube collects grit and evaporates. Well-tended chains are less likely to rust and wear. Jim Woodworth, the founder of Action Wheels in Deptford, New Jersey, recommends relubing your chain every couple hundred miles, although frequency depends on your riding conditions. With the same caveat, he suggests a more thorough cleaning via the removal of the chain and a degreasing bath every 500 miles. Woodworth founded his general-purpose bike store in his parents' basement in 1977. He was 14 and grew enamored with bicycles during a cycling boom stemming from the first Earth Day a year earlier, a growing fitness craze, and a gas crisis. His store serves some of Philadelphia's eastern suburbs, including a number of people who commute at least partly via bicycle.

Woodworth says that relubing requires a small investment in time relative to the benefits and that the process doesn't have to stain your clothing. You'll clean the chain with a small brush and rag to avoid sealing particles into the chain links, apply lube, and then wipe off the excess.

Traditional, wet lubes are oil-based. Woodworth finds that the best lubes stick evenly but aren't tacky. He says that drip bottles are more efficient than sprays, which can be difficult to pinpoint. Finish Line, Pedro's, and Tri Flow, among others, offer quality wet, oil-based products. Prices range from $5 to $8 for two to four ounces of lube. If your commute is less than 10 miles roundtrip, that should last you for well over a year. If you're of the Costco philosophy of buying, or planning to scrap your Lexus for a fleet of bicycles, you can buy 128 ounces for $63 on Amazon. Dry lubes cost about the same and are more resistant to dust and fine grit. But they are probably not the product for cities with significant rainfall—read Seattle, Portland, and most of the eastern seaboard. Dry lubes wash away more quickly than wet lubes. As for the staple of many an American garage, WD-40, Woodworth said to use it only if you don't have bike lube. "It's better than nothing," he said. "It has some nice rust prevention qualities. It's a bit of a degreaser and lube." However, he adds, "For a person who really cares about his or her bike, it's not the best."

Tuning Up

It's clear that the more you have your bike tuned up, the better it will ride and less likely it is to suffer mechanical problems. That will lead to a better bicycling experience. You'll be more likely to ride more frequently.

But what's just enough or too much? You could visit a dentist every week for a fluoride and cleaning and win the World's Best Teeth Award. Your sane friends would also charge you with overkill.

We knew anecdotally that bike stores had different opinions on the topic. Some insisted that we needed a tune-up every few months. Others were more casual, telling us to bring our bike when something was off. We decided to settle the matter scientifically. We conducted a survey. As surveys go, our efforts were not Gallup-like. We interviewed Kelly Martin, Larry Hoffman, and a mix of about 10 other mechanics and shop owners. We asked three primary questions, although we forgot to ask the third on a number of occasions. The three questions were these:

- How often should you tune your bike?

- How much should it cost?

- What are the elements of a tune-up?

We also asked most of our interviewees when bike owners should bring in new bicycles for adjustments and what problems cause the most damage. Even more informally, we asked them to prescribe light maintenance chores that could help prevent more serious issues.

Our survey found that 9 of our 12 experts recommended at least one tune-up per year. Of that group, three said that riders who logged significant mileage should consider two tune-ups, or one tune-up and a more comprehensive overhaul. Those would include some disassembly and regreasing of major parts.

What's more significant mileage? The cut-off based on our conversations seems to be at least 10 miles per day. But that also depends on weather. Riding five miles to work and back through the sunny flats of Santa Monica isn't as hard on a bike as the same distance through the humid summers and messy winters in northern latitudes. Changing seasons alone can create problems. "Each season has its own challenges," said Jonathan Morrison, a volunteer mechanic at Salt Lake City's Bike Collective.

Morrison was one of the experts who gently suggested having a semiannual tune-up, one apiece for warmer and colder months. Others felt it was best to monitor maintenance in colder months.

Michael Pappaconstantine, a bike mechanic for 28 years now based at Belmont Wheelworks in the Boston suburb of Belmont, said that cold weather isn't what wrecks bikes but rather the rain and snow and different types of particles that collect on roads. "Temperature doesn't matter," said Pappaconstantine. "It's salt and sand. The wet weather is tough. The general messiness of roads is harder on bikes."

We'd add that sea air is also hard on bikes. It corrodes steel frames and destroys seats. If you're a sea captain or own a houseboat, keep your bike inside.

The frequency of tune-ups will also depend on the quality of the bike. Pay more, and you'll have less to do because the parts and craftsmanship are of such high quality. Cheaper models tend to break down faster. Pappaconstantine said that a rider's weight is also an issue. "Bigger riders wear out drive chains faster than smaller ones," he said.

Yet our interviewees unanimously said that maintenance should be an almost daily ritual. That amounts to watching and listening, not unlike pilots who give their plane a once-over before each flight. This analogy has particular resonance given that Orville and Wilbur Wright were bicycle mechanics who used bike parts and technology to invent their plane.

A conscientious cyclist will inspect the tires. Do they look low? You'll pull out the minipump from your fool's bag. Is the chain gritty and the frame splattered with dirt and grease? It's time for the bristle brush and cleaner. Are the wheels or brake calipers straight? Is the seat angled improperly? A bike with parts visibly askew may function but not without potential long-term damage requiring costlier repairs than might be needed upon quicker diagnosis. "Get to things early and you'll alleviate more severe problems," said Kelly Martin.

At least three experts in our survey, including Bike Collective's Morrison, suggest a harsher if improbable-sounding test. Drop your bike. Just a few inches, mind you. That's enough to detect the rattle of loose or broken parts that will foreshadow bigger problems. Spin the crank and wheels, squeeze the brakes, and hop on the bike to change gears a few times. If something doesn't sound right, it probably isn't. "When you hear a new rattle, it's time to have the bike looked at," Morrison said. "It indicates that something's loose. Look for crunchy noises or vibrations that indicate there's grit where it shouldn't be."

The smart cyclist always monitors performance. Is the ride smooth? Does the bike turn easily without groans or squeaks? Does it respond to touch the way you expect? Do you feel as if your seat or riding position is shifting? Your body will detect even barely perceptible changes to seat height, leg extension, and body extension. Remember the old chestnut: if something doesn't seem right, it probably isn't.

Based on our survey, your tune-up should cost between $50 and $100. The price depends on location, with shops in bigger cities not surprisingly more on the high end. The most expensive in our survey, City Cycles in Washington D.C., charges $100, and Belmont Wheelworks charges $69 for roughly the same service as Bicycle South in Atlanta, which charges $67.50. Rasmussen Bicycle Shop in Des Moines, Iowa, and Bicycle Butler in Spokane, Washington, charge $50. City Cycles and Belmont were the most expensive in our survey, not surprising given the cost of living in those cities. Atlanta is no slouch in that department either. There are exceptions to this rule. We paid $49 for a tune-up at Safety Cycle, one of the oldest bike shops in Los Angeles. A random search of other cities found a range of prices.

What do you get for your money? Our survey found that tune-ups follow a similar checklist, albeit not always in the same order. The mechanic does the following:

- Listens for loose parts and unusual noises by spinning the parts that are supposed to spin and turning others.

- Trues the wheels to ensure that weight is being evenly distributed.

- Cleans the chain and applies lube.

- Adjusts tension on the cables for braking and shifting and checks the derailleurs and drive chain.

- Ensures the seat and handlebars are sturdy and angled properly.

- Monitors air pressure.

- Replaces faulty handles.

- Washes the frame of grit and grease.

A few mechanics speak with customers about their riding habits and routes before starting. "I like to know what people are doing," said Belmont's Pappaconstantine. The tune-up usually takes an hour to 90 minutes. Our Safety Cycle tune-up lasted nearly two hours, but our Specialized Rockhopper hadn't been to the shop in years—our bad. Better-maintained bikes won't need as much time. One more note: we watched our tune-up. Indeed, you'll often be able to watch the servicing. Repair areas are often visible. But high season may bring slow turnarounds. One survey respondent said that his mechanics were occasionally backed up a week or two in summer.

The retailers who participated in our survey all offer more comprehensive overhauls for 30 to 50 percent more. These services combine all of the just-listed services menu with a thorough disassembly, regreasing, and rebuilding of the frame. A few shops use sonic degreasers to ensure the chain is spotless.

Safety Cycle's higher-level overhaul includes the removal of the stem, seat post, and ball bearing cassettes, which enable the wheels and cranks to turn efficiently. The cost: more than $100. Some shops will offer an even more sophisticated service at higher cost. We'll spare you the details, except to say it's thorough.

As far as servicing new bicycles goes, most shops have fair policies about initial maintenance visits. New bikes require some adjustment of brakes and gears because their cables stretch in the first 100 miles or so of riding. The retailers in our survey offer a free tune-up—largely to address this issue—within the first 30 days to six months or 200 miles of riding. But even those parameters may be … stretched—ugh—in the interest of keeping customers happy. Bicycle South and Belmont have 90-day policies. "Any time between the date of purchase and 90 days we'll tell the customer we'll look at the bike while they wait," said mechanic Michael Pappaconstantine. "Cables stretch, housings tend to compress." Bicycle Butler in Spokane offers two free tune-ups in the first two years after purchase, plus a lifetime derailleur adjustment. "Mountain bikes tend to stretch faster," said Eric Schneck, a Butler mechanic.

Then there's Nechama Levy, the head mechanic at Adeline Adeline in the hip Tribeca section of New York City. Adeline Adeline specializes in city bikes, practical uprights modeled after Dutch bikes, and old-style workhorses that have returned to favor in recent years. Levy has worked on bikes since she was a teen and made a living as a mechanic for four years. "I love to work on bikes," Levy said. "It's a calling." Levy "pre–breaks-in" the store's bikes, "prestretching cables," "stress-relieving" wheel spokes so they're not carrying too much tension, and double-checking bearings and lug nuts at key points. She said that she's "protecting the bike." But Levy also feels strongly about servicing bikes in the first few weeks after purchase. "What we say is if there are problems, bring the bike back and we'll adjust it," Levy said.

Our Tune-Up and Finding the Right Mechanic

We've had good luck with bike mechanics and believe that almost all of them are passionate cyclists who live to work on bikes. What other reason would they have for spending time at low pay in small rooms with greasy work tables and lots and lots of wrenches? "It seems lame, but anyone who works as a bike mechanic just loves bikes," said Nechama Levy, the head mechanic for New York–based Adeline Adeline. Levy works down a narrow staircase in a rear basement corner. She can go hours without seeing a customer. She is intense, pierced, and rides fearlessly around New York City—in short, she is our romanticized version of a mechanic.

Alas, not all mechanics share her devotion or integrity. Bike mechanics bear a resemblance to their car- or vacuum-servicing cousins. Some are better than others, buyer beware. Based on a recent conversation with Calvin Jones, the longtime educational director for bike tools manufacturer Parktools, we'll categorize the bad into three groups:

Clock punchers: They toil without passion. They treat bike maintenance and repair as if on an assembly line, moving quickly from one job to the next, unlikely to diagnose problems outside what they've been asked to inspect. Good mechanics treat every bike as if it's their own. They're bike intellectuals—inquisitive, searching, and eager to help someone because they know a good bike enhances the riding experience. Riders should demand more than "boilerplate," said Jones. "Some mechanics care and some don't, and the latter is when trouble begins."

Fair-deal Dans or Daniellas: They see servicing appointments as opportunities to sell you more products and services. Jones cites a shop that was eager to replace a bent hanger connecting a derailleur to the frame when the part could be bent back into place. He began repairing bikes in the early 1970s and worked in a number of retail stores before joining Parktools. Jones also teaches repair at the Bicycle Institute and serves as a mechanic and consultant to the U.S. Olympic team. His philosophy about repair: scrutinize the bike and find the best, least costly option for returning it to health. "Some shops use the tune-up as a way to sell. They're concerned that they won't see the customer in a year so they want to make the most of their visit. They get excited. They hit the gas. You have to ask questions like 'Do I really need new brake pads?' Bike shops shouldn't rake you over the coals. They need to make sense. Good mechanics solve problems and aren't just parts replacers."

Incommunicados: There's a tendency among service professionals to blind you with knowledge. The worst of them simply want to impress you. They tend to speak quickly as they're spouting terminology that sounds more like Klingon than English. Others believe that everyone is as fluent in their profession's lingo as they are, while some are simply too impatient to explain what they want to do for you. There are good bike mechanics who are poor communicators. But we've already made the point that bike technology is technology with a small *t*. The design has remained roughly the same since the last decade of the nineteenth century, and problems—or costs—shouldn't be hard to explain. If you don't understand something, ask questions until you receive a satisfactory explanation. Don't let a mechanic "blow you off or say that they can't explain a repair to you," Jones said.

With larger shops, Jones advises seeking mechanics with more experience and a sense of customer service. And if you're feeling a little motivated, adopt the philosophy of the educated consumer: learn a few terms. "There's a level of bull protection," Jones said.

We kept the above in mind when we asked Diego Souza, the head mechanic for Los Angeles–based Safety Cycle, to tune up our bike. Safety Cycle, which was founded in 1940, is the oldest bicycle store in Hollywood, possibly the city. It is located in an unlikely spot for a bike retailer, on the rim of one of Los Angeles' gang-infested areas, outside corridors of college students or high-income families. But Safety Cycle has drawn a loyal clientele over the years and benefited enough from the growing interest in city cycling to double its space. Helmets and tires hang from racks. Derailleurs, brakes, and cable units fill several cases. City Cycle's stock is mainly composed of hybrids, touring bikes, and fixed-gear cycles with a few mountain bikes, fold-up Dahons, and city-style bicycles from Republic and Electra mixed in—in short, the bread-and-butter of the urban cyclist.

The 20-something, curly haired Souza is a bicycle lifer. He joined the shop in early 2010 after moving to Los Angeles from Savannah, Georgia, where he had also worked as a mechanic after years of riding in his native Brazil and the U.S. He still rides an hour or more at breakneck speeds on the fixed-gear bicycles that he builds himself. "I've been biking since I was a little kid," Souza said. "It's in my blood."

Even before taking our Rockhopper, Souza asked us how we used the bike and how frequently we rode. Several other mechanics we'd interviewed for our nonscientific survey would subsequently tell us that this was a good way to start the tune-up. It offered them clues about where they might find wear and tear. "We're always asking how often someone rides, how far, and in what weather," said Fred Boykin, the owner of Bicycle South in Atlanta.

We told him that the bike hadn't been in a shop for years and was only recently back in regular use. He mounted the bike and used a cassette brush with sharp bristles to remove grit from the chain and applied lube. Then he trued the wheels, spinning them on a truing stand and adjusting the spokes with a spoke wrench until the tension was right. The spoke wrench is one of those unique pieces of bike equipment that looks like little more than the sort of device fish restaurants give you to crack open lobster claws. "Once you have the wheels straight, the rest is a piece of cake," Souza said.

Not so fast, we thought as he disentangled pieces of packing string from the chain ring and noticed that our right shifter wasn't working properly. Souza tried to salvage the shifter, found that the main spring had broken, and recommended that we replace the unit. He also suggested replacing a frayed cable and an end cap, which had gone missing. He told us that the repairs would cost about $30 above the tune-up charge. As the local techno group Propagandi blared from an iPod, Souza replaced the faulty parts. "Try this," he said, and we pushed the new plastic lever up and down.

Then Souza added some air to the tires and cleaned the frame with a pink, biodegradable wash made by Finish Line. Souza likes Finish Line but said that there are a number of other products that clean equally well. He said that despite its irregular maintenance schedule, our bicycle was in "pretty good shape." "The chain and other major parts don't look like they're 10 years old," he said. "The problem with the shifter couldn't have been avoided with more maintenance. Sometimes parts, particularly plastic ones, wear down with time."

Our bill: about $95 including tax.

We promised to come back more frequently.

12

Accidents

How to Survive by Learning
from the Experiences of Others

We dedicate this chapter to an unlikely party.

The car driver.

You may know the driver as the person who isn't riding a bicycle or walking. Drivers in the U.S. go about 200 million strong and make up roughly 99.5 percent of America's commuters, give or take the odd tractor. Drivers, of course, come in many shapes and sizes, although we fit them into two categories.

Can they see you or not see you?

Some drivers are tall. They can see you, and as long as their judgment is intact, you don't have to worry about them. We had friends who once saw Shaquille O'Neal in his car. We would not be afraid of him not seeing us.

Some drivers are short. In fact, they are so short that you can only see the tops of their heads over the dashboard.

Big worry.

There are truckers and monster truck drivers who can't see at all because they're riding about 20' above ground. The same holds true for minivan drivers who can't see you because they're trying to prevent the five kids whom they're ferrying to ballet, art, and soccer practice from tearing each other's heads off while feeding them all snacks. There are taxicab drivers who can only see part of you because they have too many good-luck charms hanging from their rearview mirror. There are Winnebago drivers who cannot see you because they keep glancing at their Automobile Club of America map and arguing with their spouse.

Honda Civic drivers can see you because they are driving cars with configurations more along the lines of what Henry Ford intended. By the way, Ford was a bicycle mechanic before he invented the Model T.

Prius drivers will see you because they feel that they have a moral obligation to see you. They want to support cyclists who are creating an even smaller carbon footprint than they are. VW Bug, Smart, and electric car drivers will see you because their cars aren't much bigger than your bicycle. Many of them are cyclists, too.

But alas, there are also drivers who are not interested in seeing anything except a mile of clear road before them. They see cyclists, who appear as even a blip on their radar, as the enemy. These are called road ragers or, in a few cases, psychopaths. Contrary to popular belief, road ragers do not exclusively drive SUVs and pickup trucks but come in many shapes and sizes. Witness the 2010 conviction for assault with a deadly weapon (his car), battery, and reckless driving of Christopher

Thompson, a Los Angeles doctor, for intentionally braking hard so that two cyclists would plow into him. One cyclist separated his shoulder while the other broke his nose. All this resulted from someone who allegedly took the Hippocratic oath to "never do harm to anyone." Thompson was sentenced to five years in state prison.

We have already addressed some of the things that you can do to ride safer and directed you to the fine safe cycling texts of John Allen and John Forester. But manuals address only what you should do. If you're reading this book, we assume that you are responsible and will do everything in your power to do everything right.

Some drivers are another story. And we thought how better to prepare you for the rough, tough world of urban cycling than to share some of their less savory or unintentionally harmful behaviors with a word or two about how to avoid them. We rate each driving maneuver for avoidability on a scale of one to 10 spokes, with one spoke a mildly annoying event that you can skip around and 10 for circumstances that leave you almost no escape from harm. We draw examples from our own experiences and those of people we've interviewed or read about through the years.

The Intentional Right Turn to Create Mayhem

The Scenario: A car traveling in the same direction as you speeds past, makes a quick right under your wheels, and then stops suddenly, forcing you to stop short. The Intentional Right Turn to Create Mayhem, or IRTCM, usually occurs when there is a driveway or intersection without a stop sign or signal. Never mind that drivers are always supposed to defer to pedestrians and cyclists. We also occasionally call the IRTCM the taxi turn

Driveways can be a cyclist's nightmare.

in honor of the many New York cabbies who believe they have the right of way at every intersection.

The result—and often the intent—is that you hit the car and go flying or that you stop so suddenly that you go flying. The driver then drives away, perhaps looking back with a sneer. This is undoubtedly one of the toughest maneuvers for a cyclist to avoid because the driver is coming from a blind spot. Unless you're looking to make a left turn, you are usually focusing straight ahead and not to the side. Because you are a good person, you are not expecting someone to hurt you. The Intentional Right Turn to Create Mayhem, or IRTCM, is like boxing Manny Pacquiao to a standstill only to have him nail you with a sucker punch as you return to your corner between rounds.

The Solution: If you've already started crossing in front of a driveway or intersection and a driver is intent on making an IRTCM, you're in a tough spot. The car can move faster than you can react. But there are a couple of things you can do to at least partly anticipate the IRTCM. Remember that good cycling requires not only using your eyes but also your ears. Listen carefully for cars coming up fast. Take frequent glances to the side.

We don't slow up for every driveway, lest it take us two days to travel two miles. But we do tend to decelerate through intersections if we see or hear a car that seems about to draw even. In doing so, we feel a little more ready for anything bad that might happen.

Don't be lulled into a false sense of security on quiet streets. We were once cycling with a friend on a 20-mile bike path around the outskirts of Tallahassee, Florida. It was a quiet, lazy winter morning with little traffic on the road that paralleled the path. But as our friend began to cross an intersecting street, a white pickup truck wheeled in front of him and stopped. Our friend was able to stop without falling. The driver emerged from his car and stared him down. Nothing happened and the driver eventually went his way. But the experience was unsettling.

Avoidability Rating: Seven spokes

The Unintentional Right Turn That Creates Mayhem

The Scenario: Sometimes a driver behaves so surprisingly and illogically that you're not sure what he or she's thinking. We believe that this occurs simply because everyone's brain is overloaded. Overloaded by increasingly more demanding work and family obligations. Overloaded by electronic communications that beep and buzz wherever we are.

Sometimes the driver simply loses track for a split second, perhaps scrambling to answer the phone or thinking of an item not executed from a 10-page to-do list. A few years ago,

Singing + Yelling = Living

Go on. Admit it—you love singing in the shower.

No, we haven't been watching you bathe. It's simply a natural human condition to sing when in a good mood. So why rein in that urge when you're cycling? After all, singing aloud to your favorite songs just may save your life one day.

Riding in traffic requires bikes to share the roadways with cars, SUVs, trucks, construction vehicles, buses, 18-wheelers, and motorcycles, not to mention other cyclists and, of course, pedestrians.

You can attach a horn to your bike that some motorists or pedestrians may hear, or you can make your presence known the simplest way possible: yelling loudly.

We have used expensive compressed-air horns and cheap bubble horns and have found that neither really helps a bicyclist make his or her presence known. But the one surefire tactic is to use your lung capacity to yell as quickly and loudly as possible.

"I totally agree that yelling is best," said Bill Jackson, a 10-year urban cycling survivor who has ridden throughout the Midwest. "Try not to sound angry and, if you have to yell at someone, say 'Sorry' or 'Thanks' *nicely*. You'd be surprised how many times the other person just made a mistake, like we all do, and will appreciate you being nice."

Don't be shy. If you don't holler in a bad situation there's a good chance you could end up under the carriage of a truck or car. But that begs a question—will you physically be able to yell when you're tired and sucking wind?

You can, if you work on it.

A trick many riders have used may prove to be the single best tactic cyclists can employ to save themselves—singing to increase lung capacity and to get comfortable using as much of your diaphragm as possible when you are already breathing heavily from your commute.

Note: the authors strenuously stress that we do not urge riders wearing ear buds. That is the biggest health risk to yourself and those around you.

However, that doesn't mean you have to ride without music.

Part of the fun in being a cyclist is the creativity you are given to personalize your bike, helmet, and gears. Vehicles don't allow this the way bicycles do. If you plastered speakers on the outside of your car

Los Angeles cyclist and former bike retailer Larry Hoffman bounced off the front end of a car on Franklin Canyon, another of those gorgeous but challenging roads that connect different parts of the city. The driver had passed comfortably ahead but turned right suddenly into a driveway. Hoffman, who was riding downhill at a brisk 25 mph pace, figured the car would pull all the way in. Instead, the driver stopped only partway into her turn. He suddenly had no time and little room to maneuver. The shoulder led to a sheer drop-off. Hoffman careened off the car, decapitating a side mirror in the process. He escaped

people would either think you are crazy or that you are pretending to be the Blues Brothers.

One simple trick is to retrofit your helmet with an oversized pair of headphones (Skull Candy's Icon 2 headphones have proven the best in our experience) with an mp3 player Velcroed to the side of the helmet. This way we can hear every crosswalk conversation, car honk, or street noise *plus* be able to enjoy music in a safe manner.

And we sing out loud as much as possible. You may look or sound foolish. That doesn't matter. If you're going to look goofy, go all the way and sing.

On your next ride, practice how long you can sing aloud to your music while cycling at full speed. You will be surprised how quickly you run out of breath. Now imagine that you had a car about to hit you at the moment when you can barely catch your breath, much less have to speak. If you can't sing in a normal voice when you're tired, will you be able to yell loud enough so the motorist can hear you through his windows and over his conversations or radio?

Whether you sing or not, expanding your lung capacity so that you can yell, no matter how tired you are, is vital to your longevity. The next time you are halfway through an intersection and a car or truck barrels at you out of nowhere and it's only the sound of your voice yelling "Hey!" at the top of your lungs that gets the driver's attention, you'll understand precisely why lung capacity is important.

And that should be reason to sing some more.

with torn bike shorts, a bent bike, and some scrapes. The car suffered $2,600 in damage. "I rode the bike home," Hoffman said. "Guys who were riding behind me said it was the loudest crash they'd ever heard, like an explosion. The handlebars bent, but I still ride the bike. I've learned to ride with them."

The Solution: Anything we say would sound like a criticism of Hoffman, and that would be unfair. Hoffman has ridden seriously throughout Los Angeles for more than four decades. He rides carefully. He's had only this one accident in his cycling experience. Should he have slowed until the car completed the turn? Perhaps. Then again, no one can predict everything. Or to quote one of our favorite old pop singers Elvis Costello: "Accidents will happen."

Avoidability Rating: 9 spokes (We are tough graders.)

The Left Turn Cut-Off to Create Mayhem

The Scenario: This is the evil sister of the IRTCM. Consider them the Wicked Witches of the West and East. The lead-up to this event is roughly the same. You're riding along peacefully when a driver intentionally or mindlessly cuts you off at an intersection. In this instance, he or she not only doesn't signal, but gives you as little time as possible to respond. We know of this behavior firsthand via an incident in Los Angeles' Griffith Park. We were riding the last 20 yards of two-mile descent when the driver of a white pickup truck that was coming from the opposite direction turned sharply into our path. We were not riding fast. We are among a minority that doesn't like downhills. The truck didn't raise alarm bells because it was moving slowly. The turn was anything but slow, though, and when we jammed on our breaks, we did a full summersault with a half-twist over the handlebars. We escaped with only a sore collarbone and assorted scrapes and bruises.

The Solution: This may be even more pernicious because the driver knows you can see him and is more calculating about when he or she turns. We would suggest slowing down almost always when you enter an intersection.

Avoidability Rating: 7 spokes

The Stop in Front of Your Car

The Scenario: A driver, usually annoyed at having to follow the cyclist on a narrow street, sees an opening to pass. But then instead of speeding on, he jams on the brakes. The closer to the cyclist's front wheel, the more pernicious is the stop. This is more or less what occurred when Dr. Christopher Thompson assaulted two bicyclists on Mandeville Canyon, a curling, two-lane road that cuts through one of Los Angeles' most scenic residential areas and is popular with cyclists. Thompson and a few of his neighbors had tangled with cyclists for years over road-sharing issues. The residents insisted that cyclists were impertinent and purposely hindered their ability to drive

Well-maintained brakes can help you avoid accidents.

normally. Cyclists maintained that drivers were impatient and drove too quickly.

The trial drew national attention as a test of cyclists' rights, and according to a *Los Angeles Times* report, more than 270 people wrote the presiding judge to support a tough sentence for Thompson. Just four months before the accident, Thompson had allegedly tried to run two other cyclists off the road. Those cyclists were not injured. During the trial, the assault victims testified that Thompson had behaved menacingly toward them prior to the crash, and a policeman said that Thompson had told him that he wanted to teach the cyclists a lesson.

The Solution: We don't mean to sound like too big a downer, but if motorists really want to hurt you, they can. They have the advantage. They are driving bigger, faster vehicles and know what they're going to do before they do it. As a cyclist, you are in reactive mode, often with only a few nanoseconds to make a life-or-limb decision. We would again recommend listening carefully. We will assume that you have stashed your earphones and cell phone where they should be: in your bag or zip pocket. We will again urge you to look to the side frequently. Most of all, trust your instincts. If you hear a car accelerating in a way that doesn't seem normal or see the vehicle darting around like a NASCAR entrant jockeying for position at Talladega Speedway, then slow up, stop, or move to a place where you're less likely to be confronted. Then make note of the license plate and report the incident. Too many people figure that they shouldn't bother filing a police report if they aren't injured. Law enforcement will tell you just the opposite. Call the police. File the report. If someone is willing to threaten you, then they've probably tried the same thing with other cyclists. It's easier for police to do something if they have a record of malicious behavior.

Avoidability Rating: 6 spokes

The-Timing-Couldn't-Have-Been-Worse Driveway Back Out

The Scenario: Just as you cycle past, a driver backs quickly out of a hidden driveway, believing that traffic has cleared. By hidden driveway, we mean that buildings or walls have obscured the driveway entrance. In some instances the apron is difficult to distinguish from the curb because they are at roughly the same height, or because they are damaged. The TCHBWDBO is generally not an action of evil but rather carelessness, or simply because of what we call inadequate expectations. The driver has been conditioned to look for car traffic, but not for cyclists. The driver proceeds with the false confidence that everything is clear. If the driveway is on a busy street, the driver backs out with speed.

The Solution: Proceed with caution past all driveways.

Avoidability Rating: 6 spokes

Car Edging Into Your Lane

The Scenario: The driver changes lanes without realizing that the car is within striking distance of a cyclist or drifts over absentmindedly. We see this all the time and consider it a further example of mind overload. People become preoccupied with their to-do lists.

The Solution: As threatening maneuvers go, this one is easier to avoid. We will assume that you are looking ahead as you cycle and simultaneously also keeping a wary eye on cars to your left. We would remind you to stay out of blind spots as much as possible. We occasionally even try to catch the eye of drivers in the rearview mirror, or at least watch where they are looking. Clearly, a driver looking at his or her lap frequently is texting. Your warning signals should go off instantly. The driver is only partially paying attention to the road.

Avoidability Rating: 3 spokes

Keeping your eyes on nearby motorists can help prevent an accident. (J. MAUS/BIKEPORTLAND)

Garbage Truck Back Up

The Scenario: A garbage truck driver doesn't see you because he is sitting at tree branch level, and his mirrors leave blind spots. In 2006, bicycle mechanic Nechama Levy suffered crushed leg bones when a garbage truck knocked her down while backing up. Levy had been riding New York City streets for years

Not all bike lanes are meticulously marked.

without incident when the accident occurred. "They [truck drivers] drive like no else is there," Levy said.

The Solution: It's difficult to find fault with a veteran rider who could probably teach us a thing or two about urban cycling. We would merely suggest driving with greater caution around larger vehicles whose drivers sit high off the ground.

Avoidability Rating: 7 spokes

The Door Prize

The Scenario: The driver parks and then opens the door, seemingly unaware that he may clothesline a passing cyclist. We do not have statistics but believe that the Door Prize is among the most common accidents. If you're looking for deeper social significance, the Door Prize highlights cycling's relative lack of status. Most drivers don't think of cyclists as they're about to leave their car but rather of making a hasty exit. Car door extensions are one of those injustices for cyclists. You're not really paying attention to the parked cars to begin with, and there's almost no way to predict if someone is exiting a car without looking.

Beware of parked cars.

The Solution: We are going to say something ridiculously obvious, but bear with us. We recommend ensuring that you keep a more respectable distance from parked cars than you might have considered. You might also make note of who's parallel parking in the near distance. These drivers are the most likely to open their doors. Whenever possible, try also to make eye contact with drivers.

Avoidability Rating: 8 spokes

Other Scenarios

- Homicidal maniac looking for people to hit: 10 spokes.

- Grandmother with thick glasses driving at 20 mph, five miles below the speed limit on a quiet residential street: 2 spokes.

Riding in extreme weather can increase the likelihood of an accident. (J. MAUS/BIKEPORTLAND)

- Seventeen-year-old boy with a one-week-old license driving the family car: 2–10 spokes, depending on whether he's just broken up with his girlfriend.

- Seventeen-year-old girl with a one-week-old license driving the family car: 2–9 spokes, depending on whether she's speaking on a cell phone with friends.

- Hollywood star on Sunset Boulevard driving a sports car: 7–10 spokes, depending on whether the star is merely having relationship problems or about to enter rehab.

- Normal drivers in normal conditions: 1 spoke.

- Normal drivers in inclement weather: 2 spokes (4 spokes in Southern California where no one knows how to drive in rain, a ½ spoke in Portland, Oregon, where people drive in nothing but rain and love bicycles).

13

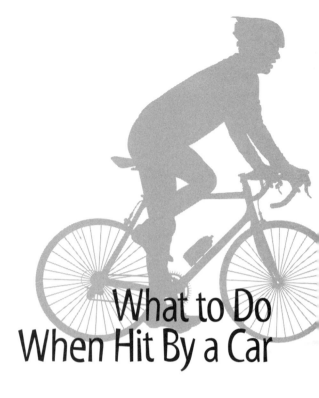

What to Do When Hit By a Car

It's finally happened—either you hit a car, a car hit you, or you were doored by someone opening his or her car door. The good news is that the worst is over and you've survived. The bad news is that you're sprawled out in the middle of a busy city street, your bike may be in pieces, and your personal possessions are strewn about the area. While this is happening, every pedestrian nearby is probably gawking at your predicament, muttering something like *That cyclist probably had it coming to him anyway.*

So what do you do now? You're in pain, embarrassed, confused, and possibly at the very beginning of a long insurance and/or legal battle.

A young cyclist falls. When you are involved in an accident, make sure to take the appropriate steps to protect yourself both physically and legally.

To help out, we've documented the steps anyone should follow if he or she is in any bicycling accident of any kind.

The first thing you need to know is that in this type of situation you must be strong and insistent. Now is not the time for being nice or cordial. That may be your instinct, to downplay someone else's fault because everyday manners have conditioned most of us to react that way. However, this is one of the most serious situations you will ever be in and being kind will only hurt you in the long run. Your attempts at politely trying to downplay the incident will be used against you by the insurance company later on if you file a claim so do not say anything that could be construed as taking blame for the accident.

When you get home, you can be nice to your family and friends.

When you're in the middle of a bicycle accident, you need to be firm and get the police and/or ambulance involved instantly.

"Outside of necessary communication, keep your statements to a minimum," advises attorney John A. Lewert of

Lake Forest, Illinois, who has worked personal injury cases for years. "As you may be at the precipice of a legal battle that you are drawn into, any statements made to the other party(ies), witnesses, or police can end up being used against you by insurance companies or in court. Refrain from any apologies. If the police get involved, politely answer the officer's questions, but never incriminate yourself by assuming blame. Act as your own advocate—don't lie, but don't volunteer tangential facts that may be against your own interest."

1. **Get Out of the Street:** Repeat after us—get out of the street, get out of the street, get out of the street. If you are in pain, remain where you are and yell for help. But if you are able to get to your feet you should do so immediately and get out of the street. Remember that other cars are likely still driving toward you. If you are in the middle of an intersection, the cars may arrive from multiple directions. Staying in the street will only get you hurt more. Get on the sidewalk immediately.

2. **Leave the Bike Where It Is:** Do not move your bike! In an ideal situation you will be able to get up off the street and get to the sidewalk (or out of traffic) and be able to leave your bike exactly where it fell so that you can take photographs of the accident in a few minutes.

3. **Injury Check:** As soon as you are out of immediate danger of being hit by another vehicle, do a quick inspection of your head, neck, shoulders, elbows, wrists, knees, ankles, and back. Are you bleeding? Is anything sore? When you flex your arms or legs can you feel joint pain? If you feel pain, ask someone to call 911. (Hint: turn to a specific person and look him or her in the eye and say,

"Please call 911 right now!" Experts say that humans are conditioned to react quicker when they have been personally challenged to act.)

4. **Call the Police:** Don't hesitate. You want a record of the accident. You need instant help. Tell the police dispatch that there are injuries, which should help get them there sooner.

5. **Get Driver's Info:** Write down the driver's license plate number, especially if the driver gives any indication that he or she is about to flee the scene. You want to collect the driver's license and insurance information. Also, get a phone number and email address. Don't be surprised if the driver does not want to share this information. You cannot force him or her to give it to you. But if you have his or her insurance information, that should be all you need if the accident is processed without any unusual circumstances.

6. **Talk to Witnesses:** Before witnesses walk away, ask if anyone saw the accident. If so, ask them to stay and speak with the police officer. If you have a camera phone, take a video of them describing what they saw. If they have to leave the scene, get their phone number and email address so that you can share it with the police. But do everything you can to ensure the witnesses remain until the police say it is okay for them to leave.

7. **Photograph Everything:** "Take exhaustive pictures at the scene of the accident," Lewert said. If you have a cell phone camera, now is the time to use it. If you do not have yours or it got damaged in the accident, ask a witness to borrow his or if he will take photographs. You

want to photograph the scene of the accident with the car and the bike in the image as well as photos of your bike, close-ups of significant damage to your bike, images of the car, images of yourself if you have injuries, and photos of the section of road or the intersection where the accident occurred. Do not assume that the insurance adjuster knows the intersection.

8. **Note Details:** If the situation turns confrontational, the driver may speed off (record the license plate number and description of the car and note any bumper stickers) or the witness may walk away (get a description of the witnesses and note which way they walked to share with the police).

9. **Call an Ambulance:** If you have any pains, especially acute or sharp pains, have someone call for an ambulance. (If the person who called 911 for the police is still on the phone, have them send an ambulance too.) If you need someone else to call 911 again, ask immediately. Even if you do not think you are seriously injured, it's a good idea to have an ambulance arrive anyway. If you end up filing an insurance claim for injuries, the insurance company is going to need proof of medical treatment. If you go to the doctor or emergency room later after the accident, you need to have records of that visit too. While it shouldn't affect the processing of your claim, delaying your doctor/hospital visit until later could raise eyebrows at the insurance company. Even if they find that you did everything correctly, it will add more work for them and delay your settlement. If you think you need medical help, it's best to get started immediately both for medical and legal reasons.

If you have any pains at all after you are hit by a car, have someone call for an ambulance. (AP IMAGES)

10. **Assess the Damage to Your Bicycle:** It takes a lot to send a bike to the scrap heap. Most parts are not only sturdy but replaceable at a relatively low cost. You may even be able to pedal home or to a repair shop, albeit with parts jerry-rigged to keep the bike functioning temporarily. Broken derailleur or derailleur hanger? Tie off the derailleur and turn your bike into a fixed gear. That said, clearly, a cracked or badly bent frame is probably beyond salvage. Consider also whether your bike is worth saving. Replacing a damaged wheel on a department store special

A broken derailleur should not signal the demise of your bike. (ISTOCKPHOTO)

may not offer as much value as purchasing new. But the same treatment on an expensive bike is likely worth the time and energy.

11. **Use "Big Brother" to Your Advantage:** "We live in a world of video surveillance," Lewert reminded. "Whether they are on street corners, parking lots, or building entrances, video cameras are everywhere. Survey the

area to ascertain whether the cameras captured the accident on video. After you've taken the aforementioned postaccident steps, don't hesitate to approach the owner of that video and request a copy. If you have identified a camera that may have captured the accident, identify it to the police officer on the scene. Ask the officer to request a copy of that video or, at least include the existence of the potential video in his or her police report."

12. **Get Officer's Contact Info:** While the officer's information should be on the police report, obtain the officer's business card or contact info. You never know when or why you will need it. But if there are problems with your case you will want to speak with the officer on the scene later.

13. **Ask the Police Questions:** Don't assume you will hear from the officer later. He is busy and this may be the only accident you were in, but it could be one of several major incidents that the officer worked that day. So you need to be sure to know what is going to happen. Ask the officer things like, "Will the driver be charged? If so, with what? If not, why?" and "When will I hear from you?"

14. **Write Accident Account:** When you return home, write your account of the accident in detail. Write down everything you recall, including comments made by the driver, witnesses, or others nearby. This may never be used by the police or the insurance agent, but it will help you collect your thoughts so that your story doesn't change when you tell it again and again to the various people you will be working with for the next two months while settling your accident.

15. **Photograph Your Injuries:** When you return home (or while waiting for the police), begin taking photos of any injuries. You cannot take too many photos, especially if your case becomes a legal mess. Also, photograph objects that were destroyed—torn backpack, broken bike parts, etc.

16. **Keep Bloody Clothes in Bag:** If you have torn or bloody clothes do not wash as they are now evidence. Put those clothes in a plastic bag and keep as evidence. If you want to wear an affected article of clothing, wait until after your settlement. If your case gets tricky, you may need those clothes to corroborate your photographs of the accident and your injuries.

17. **Photograph Your Bike:** Take as many pictures as you can. If you think your derailleur is broken, take photographs of it from every angle. Photograph parts of your bike that are broken.

18. **File Insurance Claim:** Call the driver's insurance company immediately upon returning home. It doesn't matter what time it is—leave a message stating that you were in an accident. Give the driver's full name, insurance policy number, and your contact info. If all goes well, you should have a return call the next morning at the latest. If you do not hear from the insurance company, keep calling until you have a person to speak with about the accident. The key thing here is to not waste time—do it as soon as you get home.

19. **Talk to a Lawyer:** This is a judgment call. A personal injury lawyer would love to take on almost any bike-car accident because the overwhelming majority of them favor the cyclist. If you are seriously injured or if there is

extensive damage, call a lawyer without hesitation. But if you did not need to go to the hospital, then you do not need a lawyer. However, the safest course of action is to speak with a lawyer. If you have problems with the insurance company, your lawyer can handle them better anyway. You must understand the risk you are taking— but the lawyer's fees may eclipse your settlement if you have minor injuries and only need to have your bike replaced. If you required a hospital visit or you sustained serious injuries, a lawyer will be necessary.

20. **Follow Up:** After navigating the previous steps, the most important thing is stay in touch with the insurance adjuster you've been assigned. Remain patient. It is very likely that you will feel challenged by the adjuster when discussing the claim. After all, the adjusters are on the driver's side and do not want to pay you. But they *will* pay you. That *is* what insurance is for. You will have your costs covered plus extra for pain and suffering—not much extra, but some extra. It will take about two months to work through the paperwork. Losing your temper with the insurance adjuster will likely make your settlement take longer.

21. **Show up in Court:** Liability may be depend on a courtroom outcome, cautions Lewert. At the least, you will be named a witness on the traffic citation against the driver. Show up to court on the time listed on the traffic citation so you can testify to the facts surrounding the accident. If you don't know when the initial court date is scheduled, contact the officer involved and request that information. If all matters are not resolved in the first trip to court, ensure you show up to subsequent court

dates. The prosecuting attorney should be working on your behalf and keep you appraised of court dates. Ask prosecuting attorney questions you may have. If you have hired your own attorney to assist you on the case, request that he accompany you to court. Liability of the driver, as evidenced by a court ruling, can be a valuable tool in assuring that you are made whole going forward.

22. **Don't Ditch the Bike:** Even if your bike was totaled, keep possession of the bike as long as possible. Technically, if you took money from the insurance company they now own that bike. If the insurance company wants to take the broken bike, they can. The reality is that they will never do that (how and why would they?). But the point is that if your claim becomes antagonistic, they may request the bike to spite you. And if you have thrown the bike away or given it to a charity, your claim may be canceled. Also, that broken bike still has plenty of use left in it. You can recycle parts from the destroyed bike to your new one. Or you can have the bike fixed enough for street use and make it your new "winter" bike so that the salt of the streets contaminates your junker, not the nice new one you just bought with your insurance check.

Uninsured/Underinsured Motorists

One of the worst scenarios is where you did nothing wrong, the driver was at fault, but has no car insurance. Driving without insurance is illegal in every state so the driver will be ticketed for that offense, in addition to whatever may happen because of your accident.

But that doesn't help fix or replace your bike or cover the cost of medical bills.

Clearly this is a situation that we hope you do not experience. However, the news isn't all bad; there are some tactics you can employ.

Hire a lawyer. You will need expert help to get restitution.

"If you find that the driver who was at fault in your accident didn't have insurance, in a state requiring insurance, you can report that driver to the Secretary of State, who will likely take punitive measures, including but not limited to suspending the driver's license and initiating potential criminal actions against the driver," Lewert said. "If the damages that you sustain surpass the insurance limits of the driver's auto liability insurance, take heart, the driver's homeowner's insurance policy may include riders for the coverage of your damages. An attorney working on your behalf will likely help you access potential additional insurance policies held by the driver, if it is necessary to make you whole."

Cyclists must obey the same traffic rules as drivers, including halting at stop signs. (J. MAUS/BIKEPORTLAND)

14

Cycle Rage

Learning to Share

Ziggy, the dog of one of this book's authors, consistently ignores her dozen or so toys and stuffed animals *until* anyone, regardless of species, shows the slightest interest. When that happens, she will get to her feet immediately and take back her toy aggressively before gruffly settling back down with her toy tucked in her paws.

Motorists and cyclists are apparently similar when it comes to road ownership. There are simply more people sharing the same limited amount of space that the roads offer. Complicating this fact are other factors such as impatience at the amount of traffic, the everyday stress of family and work, anger at other users of the road doing what they shouldn't, and fear that "one of those morons" will hit their car.

"The more drivers there are for the same amount of road space, the more often you have to adjust your behavior to others: slowing down, changing lanes, waiting, yielding, and so on," said Dr. Leon James, a psychology professor at the University of Hawaii and one of the leaders in the study of road rage. "Any one of these exchanges can go wrong. So the more driver exchanges there are, the more potential there is for emotions to flare up. The mini-relationships we experience with thousands of other road users every year only last a few seconds or so, yet they are very significant, very important, influencing your fate, your future, your self-respect, your pocketbook, and your morality."

James points out that all road users—motorists and cyclists alike—consider their vehicle to be an extension of themselves.

That means that any act of aggression against a person's car or bike will produce a negative reaction because the owner will feel the slight was against him or her. Two emotions—anger and fear—are at the core of what appear to be rising rates of

Mourners in Portland attend a vigil for a fallen cyclist. Their signs express a theme that both riders and motorists should keep in mind. (J. MAUS/BIKEPORTLAND)

road/cycle rage. Cyclists and motorists constantly juggle the emotions of fear (worried that someone will hit their car/bike or that someone's poor skills will make them late for where they are going) and anger (realizing that you cannot control your immediate future because of other motorists, cyclists, construction areas, etc.). That is a potentially lethal combination, especially when you factor in the ease with which a cyclist can lash out and hit a car and then be gone (known by many as "U-lock assaults" since the heavy U-lock that cyclists need for their bikes can also double as a weapon).

A recent study by the National Highway Traffic Safety Administration (NHTSA) found that 66 percent of all traffic fatalities are caused by aggressive driving (tailgating, running red lights or stop signs, passing illegally), and more than 20 million injuries have occurred since 1990. A study could not be found that chronicles the number of accidents caused by cyclists attacking vehicles. However, experienced cyclists have multiple stories of incidents with vehicles. They just don't usually get reported to authorities.

On his extensive website about road rage, DrDriving.org, James offers 14 safety principles. In the end, however, all rules point to the Golden Rule: treat others as you would like to be treated.

"All I do is remember that on my bike I am vulnerable, and this helps keep things in perspective for me," said Bryan Finigan, who has been a bike messenger, mechanic, and salesman for more than 20 years.

It is important to remember a few things:

1. Motorists and cyclists BOTH consider their vehicles to be their personal agent of freedom and a way to get away from the world.

2. Motorists and cyclists BOTH detest when their freedom is suddenly hijacked and they are stuck in traffic.

3. Motorists and cyclists BOTH react negatively when this sudden change from free to stuck occurs.

4. Motorists and cyclists BOTH will only need a small spark to turn their negative feelings into horrible physical acts if pushed enough.

So how do we avoid cycle rage?

"The safest and most intelligent behavior we can perform when in the grips of rage and hate against a motorist is to broaden our perspective on traffic and, at the same time, to maneuver effectively out of danger," said James in an interview. "This involves removing yourself from the hate and rage of the tailgater. Whatever is the quickest way you can, removing yourself from the situation is your safest and most intelligent response to the rude behavior of others in traffic.

"Resist the strong temptation to 'let the driver know how you feel' or to 'give him a piece of your mind' or some other insanity like that. Emotional intelligence as a cyclist will save your life and your sanity. The sane point in traffic is to get away from trouble, not to face it and oppose it.

"When in traffic do not get involved in the idea of justice for cyclists who are mishandled by inconsiderate and aggressive drivers. That is the wrong thing to do, in the wrong place, at the wrong time, under wrong conditions. If you escape from an incident without injury, as is the case with most routine incidents, keep going and feel lucky. Do not look for justice or revenge. Do not engage or communicate with the wrong-doer. Get away. Be happy. Continue your life. Don't give the wrongdoer the power to suddenly change your day or your life. Get away and get free, and continue your life."

Some cities have heeded James' basic point—that you avoid trouble by creating better roadways for cyclists and motorists to share. San Francisco and other communities have begun creating "bicycle boulevards" that seek to mimic the success that many other countries around the world have employed for years, giving bicyclists their own area to ride to reduce the interaction between cars and bikes.

"You can see this kind of systems approach in the bicycle boulevards in Berkeley," said Tim Mollette-Parks, a California-based urban designer and visiting lecturer at UC Berkeley. "While not perfect, the way the bicycle boulevards allow cyclists to connect from the larger Bay Trail to downtown, all the while providing connections to mass transit, it really makes the most of the overlapping systems. And while the cyclists typically do have to share the street with cars along

San Francisco and other cities created "bicycle boulevards," giving bicyclists their own area to ride to reduce the interaction between cars and bikes. (CARRIE CIZAUSKAS)

these boulevards, much is done to increase the safety, visibility, and ease for cyclists. For example, many of the streets have bicycle-only access points, creating streets that are dead-end and slow moving for cars, but flow-through and quicker for bikes. Also, the Berkeley boulevards have very clear, overscaled street markings for bicycle lanes, which have gone a long way toward improving how bikes move through the city and their prominence in the minds of drivers and pedestrians."

Mollette-Parks is also optimistic about future city designs because of the role that newer automobiles play. While Americans have always loved large cars, there is no denying the trend toward hybrid vehicles, and the popularity of city cars, like the diminutive Smart Car or Mini Cooper. "That is good news for bicyclists as city developers and engineers look toward improving overall city design," Mollette-Parks said.

"Another aspect that is really interesting is that cars are changing—they are becoming smaller, quieter, less polluting," said Mollette-Parks. "And with the cost and scarcity of fuel, that will likely continue. But our ideas of good street design have been based on large cars from the auto boom of the 1950s. Think of the broad parkways, like some of those in Chicago, that dedicate so much space to auto traffic with an overscaled lawn/tree area running between the two traffic directions. Those dimensions and the concept behind them were really about protecting residential areas from feeling the effects of large, polluting automobiles. But now, those cars are changing. What's more, those broad lawns are not very functional and are honestly a waste of irrigation water. So, a question to ask is how can these types of streets begin to be retrofitted to match the new realities of automobiles and bikes? Can we reconsider the dimensions of existing streets in the future, to reduce the space offered to cars and increase what's made available to cyclists and storm water management, instead of auto lanes that are too large and lawns that go unused?"

Julian Sayarer, who set the world record for quickest circumnavigation of the world on a bicycle in 2009 by going 18,050 miles in just 165 days, said that he definitely noticed changes in his road rage depending on which country he was riding in. Sayarer cited Italy and France as being "cycling Meccas." He found riding there easier because the countries created bicycle-friendly roads decades ago. That has fostered better relationships between motorist and bicyclist.

"In countries where cyclists are supposed to be protected as part of a very powerful culture of road safety, I can get massive road rage against other road users and have found myself hitting wing mirrors and certainly shouting quite aggressively at drivers," Sayarer admitted. "I obviously wouldn't advocate this approach, but at the same time, the damage you can do to a car is far less than a car can do to a cyclist, so I wouldn't criticize anybody too heavily for what they do in the heat of a moment. As a general rule, I, of course, promote the diplomatic approach of keeping your wits and calm about you, but so much of the mistreatment of cyclists on roads comes from motorist ignorance of what it is that they subject cyclists to. They just drive as if we're not there sometimes, and I think it can serve a healthy role to make them aware, with restraint, of just how angry, flabbergasted, and scared you were by what has just been done without the driver perhaps even realizing."

It will take years if not decades for bicycle boulevards and other bike-friendly initiatives to become more popular in the United States. Americans seem to pride themselves on their SUVs and large cars because, if James' theory about the correlation between a vehicle and its owner is correct, Americans think that having a big car means they are a big person. It is unlikely that this sentiment will change anytime soon.

So a cyclist's biggest attribute, aside from an easygoing personality, is an ability to select routes that reduce interaction with motorists.

Even if the interaction with a vehicle that led to a road rage moment wasn't your fault, if you had selected a different street, the incident may never have happened.

By knowing the roadways and traffic patterns of areas where you ride, you can select the best roads. One of the worst things a cyclist can do is riding on roads that aren't conducive for bicycle traffic. That is asking for trouble.

15

Diary of a Commute

How to Survive by Learning from One of Our Commutes

In our ongoing quest to prove scientifically that cycling is superior to driving, we decided to test our hypothesis. We wanted the best possible proof to override any doubts of the most ardent, car-favoring cynics. We created a real-world challenge: driving versus riding.

May the best mode of transportation win.

We decided to drive a route one day and cycle the same stretch the next. To ensure that we met the standards of distinguished social and scientific journals, we set almost exactly the same conditions. We road our course at the same time on successive days, followed the same routines, carried nearly identical loads—our brown Jansport day backpack—and wore similar clothing. We rode on days with similar weather. In Southern California this is not hard. Remember Steve Martin's lazy television weatherman who never replaces the suns on his weatherboard?

To ensure that drivers wouldn't accuse us of bicycle bias, we cycled at normal speed. We obeyed the rules of the road, stopping at lights and stop signs, slowing slightly at driveway aprons, and signaling for turns. To ensure that cyclists didn't think that we were overcompensating to please the automobile crowd, when we drove, we stayed within a couple of miles of the speed limit and followed traffic rules—no Hollywood, rolling stops at stop signs.

Most of all, to ensure that our experiment resonated with the widest possible audience, we chose a route that we tackle regularly. We wanted the test to come straight from daily conditions. We felt this was good science.

We'll be submitting our journal article to the National Institutes of Something-or-Other someday.

A Ride to School

The first things you need to conduct a proper test-commute to school are a kid and a school. The kid should be of two-wheel cycling age. We have nothing against training wheels, but we wanted to complete our ride before lunch. Fortunately, an 11-year-old, whom we know well, has been riding two-wheelers since he was four—he was precocious. On top of that, he'd been eager to cycle to school. We scanned weather reports to ensure that Southern California's annual winter rains were over and awoke early enough to ensure a stress-free test.

Our route from home to school is 2.3 miles. That's front door to the sidewalk where parents drop off and pick up children. The route includes one long downhill along the narrow, chopped-up streets in our neighborhood and navigation of one of Los Angeles' prettiest, but for cyclists, scariest, four-lane

Author and son make the final right turn on the commute to school.

boulevards. It covers one final short but taxing uphill climb to
campus. We made one allowance for safety, bypassing much
of the four-lane boulevard. We sometimes do this anyway so it
did not skew our results. We drove Wednesday and Thursday
because we know that traffic is heavier the days before and
after a weekend. We left a few minutes before 8:00 AM on our
cycling day and a few minutes after the hour when we drove,
but this also did not affect conditions. We included one pit
stop for donuts on both days. Yes, we know donuts are not on
any list of healthy foods. But we sometimes stop for a donut,
and we had a hankering for the sugar glazed.

The only difference in our experiences was that our 11-year-
old companion did not cycle with his books. He normally
carries them in a red Zuca, a square, rolling suitcase that in
recent years has been the rage among elementary and middle
school students. The Zuca was simply too bulky to cart safely
on a bike. His grandmother brought the books, meeting us

shortly after arrival. You can score load hauling in the car's favor, although we believe that our companion would have been able to carry his books in a backpack.

We present now the results with a blow-by-blow account of our experience.

Driving

Time on the Road: It took us nine minutes to drive to school. This is consistent with our school drive times over the past seven years. Interestingly, we have noticed an increase in traffic and our drive time over the past two years. When we first started at our school, the commute took closer to eight minutes most days. But our experience dovetails with a steady increase nationally in commuting times over the past two decades. According to the Texas Transportation Institute, annual delays for commuters have roughly tripled since the early 1980s. In 2009, the average U.S. motorist spent 34 hours waiting out traffic congestion. Washington, D.C., and Chicago topped the rankings as the worst commuter towns. Drivers there spend 70 hours a year navigating delays. That's nearly two business weeks. Los Angeles placed fourth. Drivers there faced delays totaling 63 hours. (That represents a marked improvement from the previous few years, although we've yet to notice the difference on our area streets.) The Texas Institute, a research group based out of Texas A&M University, calculates the amount of time drivers spend commuting. Its most recent data is for 2009.

Donut Detour: We stopped for two minutes, enough time for a quick hello to the 90-something lounge pianist who presides at a corner table every morning. We'd heard that he'd been sick but he looked ready for a gig. We ordered sugar-glazed and coconut donuts.

Parking: It took us nearly four minutes from the time we passed through the school gates to the time our companion was rolling his book-laden Zuca to class. Drop-off at school is always a chore. It requires parents to wait in a line that occasionally snakes onto the street for almost a quarter of a mile. Many other Los Angeles schools face similar traffic snarls, or worse.

Total Commute Time: It took us 15 minutes, and we arrived roughly six minutes before class. We've always found the short commute one of the advantages of our school. We know many parents whose commutes are two and three times longer. We appreciate not being in a car for too long. We believe that our children are better off, too. We know that while some other kids are being ferried somewhere, ours are already engaged in an activity. Long commutes have additional costs. The Texas Transportation Institute calculates that extra costs related to commuting delays totaled $115 billion, about $808 per commuter. You can buy a slick city bike or mountain bike for the latter. Commuter delays wasted nearly four billion gallons of fuel.

Additional Notes: School commuting can be a harried experience of rushed breakfasts and forgotten homework. Sometimes shoes aren't laced until everyone is already in the car. Sometimes we have to make a quick U-turn to retrieve forgotten homework. However, on the driving segment of our two-day test, we ate a good breakfast at a comfortable pace and had the car packed in a timely manner.

Cycling

Time on the Road: It took us 18 minutes to cycle to school. We might have made it faster, except we missed one long light by seconds, and we didn't think it would be proper cycling education, not to mention safe, to cross as the light was changing red.

It took nearly 90 seconds for the light to turn green. We also rode a little more on sidewalks than we might otherwise. We felt that this was reasonable, given the age of our companion and amount of traffic we were seeing.

Donut Detour: It took us just under four minutes to receive our order of two sugar-glazed donuts and a toasted bagel with butter. We ordered the bagel because we knew that we were going to make it to school on time. We exchanged nods with the 90-something lounge performer.

Parking: It took us three minutes from the time we entered school grounds, locked the bikes to a bicycle rack, and saw our companion rolling his Zuca toward class. We might have been faster, except we had trouble arranging the bikes efficiently and threading our cable lock through the frames.

Total Commute Time: It took almost 25 minutes to cycle to school. We believe that, as we grew more comfortable cycling, and without the extended donut pit stop, we would complete

Author and son pedaling up the street to the school's main entrance.

the trip and have the bikes locked in closer to 18 minutes. We believe that we will do even better than that when our companion reaches his middle teen years. Then again, we might slow him down.

Additional Notes: We appreciated the school's two bike racks conveniently located at the top of the driveway in a spot where we could escape traffic quickly. The position of the racks, well within school grounds, would also make bicycles difficult to steal. We do not know of any bikes stolen from our school's property. The preparations at home were a little rushed, but we awoke late.

Observations

The cycle commute took 10 minutes longer than driving to school. We arrived at roughly the same time both days, and with a minimum of stress. On both days, we remained on school grounds for a few minutes, checking email and making business calls from our iPhone. We believe that the cycling experience was worth the 10 minutes that we lost—if *lost* is the right word.

Consider the upside. In those 10 minutes, we did something for our cardiovascular fitness. We burned 200 to 300 calories. We had time for conversation and observations about neighborhoods we normally see in quick glances through tinted windows. We decreased our carbon footprint. Most of all, we made a child very happy. That translates to good days at school and work.

We could rhapsodize about other smaller boons of cycling like not joining the lineup of stressed parents waiting for traffic to move and spending time outside. We felt so good when we cycled that instead of returning to our desk immediately we stopped at a favorite coffee hangout—very good for a glazed donut. We hadn't been there for a while, because every time we'd been in the vicinity, we felt rushed. That's a counterintuitive part of driving, namely the faster you go, the more rushed you feel. Sometimes from a cramped driver's seat, sealed off from the world, it feels like it would take too long to park. When you're already outside, you remove barriers.

Other Rides and Commutes

Through the months of researching this book, we joined cyclists on some of their usual rides. These rides were of a less scientific nature. We didn't record minutes on the road or time needed for locking our bike. We didn't worry about weather conditions or analyzing our thoughts riding and driving the same route. We cycled several times to pick up groceries from local stores. On one occasion, at our butcher, we had the awkward situation of not finding a convenient place to lock our bike. We leaned it near the front entrance and ordered steaks with one eye on our front wheel.

We commuted with Jonathan West on his daily seven-mile journey from Glendale to Hollywood. We navigated several wide boulevards filled with cars, many of them going too fast. West's route also requires crossing an exit ramp from the massive Interstate 5 freeway, which bisects the state of California from north to south. Cars are still traveling at highway speed as they reach the surface street, and drivers clearly aren't expecting to see a cyclist waiting to merge. West taught us good lessons about riding safely and politely in traffic. For example, he patiently reminded us to move to the center of the right lane at intersections and then move back after crossing through.

We commuted with Kelly Martin on her roughly three-mile trek to the Bicycle Kitchen. Martin took us on a postcommute tour of areas in Hollywood where she has ridden for years.

Most of them weren't bike friendly. But Martin showed us a tree-lined street that Los Angeles cyclists are hoping the city will one day convert to a bikes-only throughway. It would be ideal for bikes. But we're not expecting any change soon. Convincing cities to add resources for bicycles still takes time.

We cycled with our neighbor, Matthew Butterick, to his favorite breakfast burrito joint. The route from Hollywood to Burbank is one of the most scenic among American cities. It rises more than 1,000 feet in Griffith Park and oversees grand vistas of the Los Angeles basin on one side and the Angeles Mountain Range on the other. It took us about 50 minutes to reach out destination, about four times what it would take by car. But the time flew by.

Cycling has that effect.

Appendix

Resources

How to Survive by Having the Right Things to Read

INTERNET

Its spooky targeted advertisements not withstanding, we like Google as much as the next person for cycling information. Want to know double-time the hours of your favorite bike shop, product specs, or an updated map of cycling lanes in Chicago, and there's no better resource. Click *enter* and receive a gazillion results in nanoseconds. Desktop. Laptop. Blackberry. iPhone. At home. On the road.

But it gets tricky if you're looking for something reliably informative of a more comprehensive nature. Run a search on "bicycling gear repair," and you'll find 2.1 million places to go. Punch return on "bicycle injuries," and you'll generate 3.5 million options. Remember Jack Nicholson's Joker in the otherwise unremarkable Tim Burton version of *Batman*

(Okay, we liked Burton's Gothic vision of Gotham)? "Who ya going to trust?" the Nicholson Joker asks Gotham's citizens before gassing them and goading Batman into the film's climatic showdown.

Who indeed.

Many of us know that first entries stem from serendipitous arrangements or mastery of algorithms leading to the right position of search words. Sites hitting the optimum combination (or paying some algorithm Yoda handsomely) appear first.

But do contributors to an obscure website or video library have the chops to tell you what you should be doing about faulty shifting or pannier installation? Even if they do, can they explain it in a way that's easy to understand? The world is filled with well-meaning experts. Your time is limited. You want reliable information fast.

We ask you then to consider this section a point in the right directions, sonar in the electronic maelstrom. We list favorite websites shortly.

We have visited them the same as you might, seeking quick solutions to common problems. We include them because they've impressed us in some regard. Many may ring familiar. They've drawn sizeable audiences for years because they are user friendly. People are finding what they need.

That said, we encourage you to follow the advice offered by most smart consumers. Judge for yourself every time you use the service. If the organization of the webpage is confusing, if an article isn't answering your questions or seems questionably sourced, go elsewhere. Then don't forget to share. We are always seeking new resources.

SheldonBrown.com

The website bears the name of the widely respected West Newton, Massachusetts, bicycle mechanic. Sheldon Brown was webmaster and technical consultant for the popular Harris Cyclery. He died in 2008, but his wife, colleagues, and repair guru John Allen have continued updating it. The website provides a vast glossary of bike terms and in-depth information about repair, maintenance, and other issues.

BikeLeague.org

The League of American Bicyclists is the leading national advocacy group for cyclists. It advertises a membership of about 300,000 people. The organization produces an annual survey of the country's most bike-friendly cities. It also has information about safe riding and a wealth of other topics.

NBDA.com

The website of the National Bicycle Dealers Association offers the latest data on bicycle sales and other trends. NBDA.com's Shopping for a Bike section offers tips for buying a bicycle and accessories. The site will also help you find a shop in your area via a search engine.

Bike Snob

The Bike Snob blog is irreverent, occasionally vulgar. But like Bike Snob's large, loyal following we wait eagerly for his next observations about bicycling and society.

Twisted Spoke

San Francisco–based Matt Walsch endearingly started his blog with the hope of turning his passion for professional road racing into a career writing about the world's great races. Many of his items cover stories and personalities of interest largely to fellow fans. But Walsch occasionally veers from his sweet spot. Last year, he wrote about a bamboo bicycle, and he connects to a range of other blogs. His list of the top 10 things he's learned about blogging is sweetly confessional.

Bikeradar.com

The website belongs to Future Publishing, a leading British media company with more than 150 magazine titles. They include three of the UK's best-selling bicycle magazines, including *Mountain Biking UK* and *Cycling Plus*. The latter addresses a general audience and bears a strong resemblance to Rodale's *Bicycling* magazine. Bikeradar draws on the magazines' expertise in such areas as gear and maintenance but also covers issues of interest to urban cyclists on either side of the Atlantic, not to mention the Pacific, Indian Ocean, or Mediteranean Sea.

Bikely.com

Bikeradar's offshoot, Bikely.com, is a blessedly simple website that allows riders worldwide to download favorite and memorable biking routes. The site highlights the route on a Google map that becomes part of an archive reachable in two or three clicks from the homepage. Urban cyclists may find more stimulating alternatives to their usual neighborhood rides or the most scenic route through Durban—South Africa. Visitors who wish to participate must become Bikely members, but joining takes only a few minutes and is free.

Bicycling.com/Blogs

This site covers news and information and connects to about 30 other blogs. Our favorite names are MudandCowbells, a blog about cyclocross, FatCyclist, a generalist cycling site, and

The Mongolia Chronicles and Unholy Roleur sites, ranging in many directions.

BikeForums.net
We're not much for the forums that seem to exist for every one of the world's activities. But we know others who enjoy trading news, gossip, and other information. Many of the threads can be useful. Beware addictions!

Google Maps/Bikes
In 2010, Google unveiled a handy addition to its Maps section that allows users to map out their bike route and get directions specifically for cyclists, not motorists.

Mapmyride.com
This site was the precursor to Google's bike directions addition. You need to register, but if you intend to cycle in unknown urban locations this is another good site to use for planning ahead.

BOOKS
If you're taking time to bike, you're probably a reader who makes time for the slow, satisfying slog of book reading. We see your bookcases and night tables filled with significant volumes. Bike literature is a small genre that falls into three occasionally overlapping categories: how-to, knowledge, and entertainment. The how-to books will tell you how to buy a bike, select accessories, conduct maintenance and repairs, get in shape, and ride faster, safer, and with greater style. Knowledge books cover the best places to ride and history. Entertainment is anything else and includes some top-notch sports literature. In the list that follows we don't intend to cover everything—we

apologize for the gems we've overlooked—but to identify a few of our favorites.

Bike Snob: Systematically & Mercilessly Realigning the World of Cycling

Eben Weiss joined the list of successful bloggers turned authors. The former bike messenger and literary agent began writing an edgy, New York–cycling blog in 2007 under the pen name Bike Snob. But his common-sense observations about cycling culture and other topics resonated loudly beyond the Northeast. *Bicycling* magazine hired him to write a regular column, and his devotees include Lance Armstrong.

Major: A Black Athlete, a White Era and the Fight to Be the World's Fastest Human Being

Former *Outside* magazine editor Todd Balf's biography of the groundbreaking and ultimately tragic African American cyclist Major Taylor is among the best sports books in recent memory. Balf writes about an era in the late nineteenth and early twentieth century when man's historical quest to go faster focused on the bicycle and races in the world's first velodromes—most based in cities—drew tens of thousands of fans. For the better part of a decade, Taylor, the son of a slave, dominated his sport, becoming the world's first significant professional black athlete years before Jack Johnson won the heavyweight boxing title and decades before other major sports were integrated.

Bicycle: The History

David Herlihy is widely considered the foremost authority on bicycle history. His beautifully illustrated, densely written opus is the sort of book you can pick through on lazy weekend afternoons. *Bicycle* traces the bike's nineteenth-century origins in France and England to recent inventions that seem more in line with scenes from *The Jetsons* or *Megamind*. Herlihy has combed newspaper archives, museums, and libraries for seemingly every scrap, every detail about bicycling over the past 150 years. He also offers a convincing argument that Pierre Lallement was the true inventor of the modern bicycle.

Effective Cycling
For more than three decades, John Forester has been among the most important cycling advocates in the U.S. *Effective Cycling* is a comprehensive look at the bicycle, maintenance, and safe riding.

Bicycling Street Smarts
John Allen's thin guidebook on safe cycling is perhaps the most circulated books on cycling. It is informative, clearly written, and doesn't take up much room on a bookshelf.

The Practical Cyclist
Longtime bicycle commuter and columnist Chip Haynes writes an endearing guide for novice and average cyclists. Haynes covers the basics: bike buying, repair, accessories, and outfitting.

Pedaling Revolution
Author Jeff Mapes is a longtime reporter and columnist for the *Oregonian*. He examines the growing U.S. bike culture. The book is thoroughly reported and well written. Mapes even journeyed to Holland as part of his research.

Bicycle Mania Holland
Photojournalist Shirley J.S. Agudo's pictures are alone worth the price of the book. We see the bike-crazy Dutch cycling

through fields of sheep, along canals and dikes, on ice and at the beach. We see them toting groceries, dogs, and children. We see them riding solo and in tandem, clothed and naked. The Dutch have bicycle mania. The book's text includes a statistical analysis of Holland's bike love affair.

Copenhagen City of Bicycles

Copenhagen may or may not be second to Amsterdam as Europe's—and possibly the world's—most bike-friendly city. This book is filled with beautiful photographs of the Danes on bikes. Our favorite picture is on page 50. It shows a jam-up of cyclists waiting patiently for a light to change. The book is written in English for those of you who don't speak Danish.

The Complete Do-It-Yourself Bike Book: Everything You Need to Know to Fix, Maintain and Get the Most Out of Your Bike

British bicycle mechanic Mel Allwood has written regularly on cycling for a number of publications. Her book is useful for the beginning and more experienced cyclist. She covers bike basics, includes sections on commuting, teaching children to ride, and convincing a business to be more supportive of cyclists. Her solutions for common bike problems are well-explained and supported by color photographs.

The Lost Cyclist

David Herlihy weighs in again with a gripping adventure story of the disappearance of one of the world's great nineteenth-century high-wheel racers, and the search to determine his fate. Frank Lenz vanished on the final leg of his two-year attempt to bicycle around the world. Another cyclist, William Sachtleben, tried to learn what happened to him.

Bicycling Magazine books

Over the years, the country's leading magazine on bicycling has produced a number of excellent books. Some are focused on serious cyclists. Others have a more general bent and would be of use to cyclists of all stripes. We keep a copy of the magazine's *1,000 All-Time Best Tips* handy. We like thin books with information that is easily accessible. This book delivers on both counts.

MAGAZINES

We are regular readers of *Bicycling* magazine and *Bicycle Times*, which offer practical information for the commuter. We recently picked up *Momentum*, a Canadian publication that focuses on commuters and regular cyclists. The British publication *Boneshaker* is more artsy than informative. But we support any new publishing effort.

About the Authors

James Rubin is a Los Angeles –based journalist. He has written for the *Wall Street Journal*, the Economist Group, Forbes.com, Bankrate.com, *Los Angeles Magazine*, and other regional and national publications.

A former nationally ranked tennis player and graduate of the Columbia Graduate School of Journalism, he rides his 10-year-old Specialized mountain bike largely through scenic Griffith Park and the surrounding Hollywood Hills and Los Feliz.

Scott Rowan began bicycling daily for all his commuting and transportation needs year-round in 2004. While logging more than 15,000 miles on city streets in Chicago and other cities, Rowan has experienced every conceivable form of bicycle accident without a major injury and has only totaled a bike once—when he was doored in 2007.

Scott has worked in professional sports since 1995 as a reporter, editor, and producer of sports content for newspaper, radio, television, DVD, CD, feature films, and full-length documentaries.

Scott is divorced and lives in Chicago's Wrigleyville neighborhood with his dog, Ziggy.